SHE WAS AYE WORKIN'

Memories of Tenement Women in Edinburgh and Glasgow

My mother was always washin', always cleaning, she was aye
workin'. She never got anywhere. That was her life.
Flora MacDonald

SHE WAS AYE WORKIN'

Memories of Tenement Women in Edinburgh and Glasgow

Helen Clark and Elizabeth Carnegie

Foreword by Elaine C. Smith

White Cockade
in association with
The People's Story, City of Edinburgh Council, and
the People's Palace, Glasgow City Council

Published by

White Cockade Publishing
71 Lonsdale Road
Oxford OX2 7ES
Tel. 01865 510411
www.whitecockade.co.uk

in association with

The People's Story, City of Edinburgh Council and
the People's Palace, Glasgow City Council

First published 2003; reprinted 2003, 2004, 2006

British Library Cataloguing-in-Publication Data
A catalogue record for this book is available from the British Library.

ISBN 9781 873487 05 1 paperback

Editing and design by Perilla Kinchin
Typeset in Monotype Photina
Printed and bound in Great Britain by the Alden Press Ltd, Oxford

Front cover: Women collecting water from an outside source in Sandport Street, Leith, 1926. (Edinburgh City Libraries)
Back cover: A family in a Glasgow tenement room, c.1930. (Glasgow City Council [Museums])
Opposite title page: 1. The women and children from a stair in Victoria Place, Newhaven, late 1920s. (City of Edinburgh Museums and Galleries)

For our mothers and grandmothers

Helen Clark has been since 1985 Keeper of Social History for Edinburgh City Museums. During this time she has worked on setting up two new museums – The People's Story and Newhaven Heritage Museum – both of which use oral history extensively as a method of interpreting the past and giving members of the local communities a voice.

Elizabeth Carnegie is a graduate of Edinburgh University and Leicester University's Museums Studies programme. From 1991–8 she was a curator of social history at Glasgow Museums, where she managed the People's Palace and coordinated oral history projects. She is currently a lecturer in cultural tourism at Napier University, Edinburgh.

Elaine C. Smith, who lives in Glasgow, has become one of Scotland's most recognised performers. She has appeared regularly on television (most recently in *2000 Acres of Sky*), on radio and in live performances.

Contents

Acknowledgements

Our thanks go to all the contributors, for without their memories this book would not have been possible; to Elaine C. Smith for writing the foreword; to staff at the Living Memory Association, Edinburgh for scanning photos; to staff at Glasgow Museums for providing material and locating photos; and to Perilla Kinchin for her enthusiasm, encouragement and patience when working with the authors and her commitment and expertise in shaping and editing the text.

Illustration Acknowledgements

Photographs are copyright of City of Edinburgh Museums and Galleries (CEMG) and Glasgow City Council (Museums) (GCCM) unless otherwise indicated. Numbers refer to illustration numbers:

1 CEMG; 2 GCCM; 3 Richard Roger; 4 CEMG; 5 Edinburgh City Libraries; 6 CEMG; 7 CEMG; 8 CEMG; 9 Glasgow City Archives; 10 CEMG; 11 CEMG; 12 Glasgow City Archives; 13 GCCM; 14 GCCM; 15 CEMG; 16 CEMG; 17 CEMG; 18 GCCM; 19 CEMG; Glasgow City Archives; 21 Glasgow City Archives; 22 GCCM; 23 CEMG; 24 CEMG; 25 CEMG; 26 CEMG; 27 GCCM; 28 CEMG; 29 GCCM; 30 CEMG; 31 CEMG; 32 GCCM (photo John Thomas); 33 GCCM; 34 GCCM; 35 CEMG; 36 CEMG; 37 GCCM; 38 GCCM; 39 CEMG; 40 CEMG; 41 GCCM; 42 CEMG; 43 GCCM; 44 GCCM; 45 GCCM; 46 CEMG; 47 CEMG; 48 GCCM; 49 CEMG; 50 CEMG; 51 CEMG; 52 CEMG; 53 CEMG; 54 GCCM; 55 Springburn Museum; 56 CEMG.

Contributors

Contributors' names with place of residence and year of birth where known.

Annie Anderson, Newhaven, 1906
Barbara Anderson, Edinburgh, 1910
David Anderson, Edinburgh, 1904
Phemie Anderson, Leith, 1931
John Barnes, Leith, 1909
Emily Batten, Leith, 1917
Mima Belford, Leith, 1918
Meg Berrington, Leith, 1913
Charlie Beskow, Leith, 1916
Mary Blackie, Glasgow, 1910
Agnes Boyd, Leith, 1903
Mrs Bruce, Leith, 1905
Anne Campbell, Glasgow, 1954
Jessie Campbell, Edinburgh, c.1935
Norrie Campbell, Edinburgh, 1912
May Carson, Glasgow, 1910
Margaret Christie, Glasgow, 1920s
Greta Connor, Leith, 1927
Dolly Conroy, Glasgow, c.1915
Hannah Cowe, Leith, 1909
Joan Croal, Edinburgh, 1930
Margaret Cruickshank, Glasgow, 1920s
Nora Cruickshank, Glasgow, 1920s
Cathy Cullen, Glasgow, 1920
Margaret Cullinan, Edinburgh, 1927
Stella Curry, Glasgow, 1950
Alf Daniels, Glasgow, 1920
Councillor Davidson, Glasgow, 1909
Elizabeth Dawn, Glasgow, 1900
Mabel Dawson, Edinburgh, 1915
Cathy Dodwell, Glasgow, c.1920
William Drever, Leith, 1920
Helen Dunbar, Edinburgh, 1940
Alexander Dunnet, Leith, 1903

Madge Earl, Edinburgh, 1910
Agnes Elder, Edinburgh, c1935
Mrs Fairbairn, Leith, 1915
George Flannigan, Edinburgh, 1920
Rita Flannigan, Edinburgh, 1920
Isa Flucker, Leith, 1915
Alexander Forbes, Leith, 1914
Elizabeth Freel, Leith, 1908
Lise Friedman, Glasgow, 1930
Mrs Gardiner, Leith, 1882
Catherine Gay, Edinburgh, 1918
Mr Gibson, Leith, 1924
Mary Gilchrist, Edinburgh, 1921
Richard Goodall, Leith, 1919
James Stuart Grahame, Leith, 1906
Marald Grant, Glasgow, 1900
George Hackland, Newhaven, 1920
Thomas Hare, Leith, c.1910
Jean Hay, Edinburgh, 1914
Betty Hepburn, Edinburgh, 1920
Margaret Hepburn, Edinburgh, 1910
Alice Hick, Leith, c.1933
Mary Holligan, Edinburgh, 1910
Chrissie Hollinsworth, Leith, 1910
Mary Hutchison, Edinburgh, 1915
Ina Hutton, Edinburgh, 1906
May Hutton, Glasgow, c.1930
Mrs Inglis, Leith, 1897
Mrs Jamieson, Leith, 1925
Stanley Jamieson, Leith, 1923
Mary Johnston, Newhaven, 1926
Dodo Keenan, Leith, 1919
Alex Kellock, Glasgow, 1924
Beth K., Glasgow, 1957
Mary K., Glasgow, 1927
Isa Keith, Edinburgh, 1919
Liz Kent, Glasgow, c.1910
Bert Keppie, Edinburgh, 1924
Kulwinder Kusbia, Glasgow, 1949

Betty Laing, Glasgow, 1930
Cathy Lighterness, Newhaven, 1938
Flora Lindsay, Edinburgh, 1910
Dr Lunan, Glasgow, c.1940
Joan M., Glasgow, 1910
Molly M., Glasgow, c.1934
Norma M., Glasgow, 1920
Flora MacDonald, Edinburgh, c.1915
Margaret McDonald, Glasgow, 1950
P. McG., Glasgow, 1960
John McGowan, Glasgow, 1930
Marion McIntosh, Glasgow, 1949
Dr Mack, Glasgow, 1930
Annie McKay, Edinburgh, 1916
Mary MacKay, Edinburgh, 1929
Gertie McManus, Edinburgh, 1919
Ella McMillan, Glasgow
Mary McPhater, Glasgow, 1912
Mary Martin, Glasgow, 1920
Frances Milligan, Newhaven, 1908
Cathy N., Glasgow, 1954
Helen Nickerson, Leith, 1916
Robert Noble, Leith, 1917
Sandy Noble, Newhaven, 1908
Nan P., Glasgow, c.1920
Jane Patterson, Edinburgh, 1919
Jimmy Phillips, Glasgow, c.1930
John Preston, Leith, 1915
Christine Quarrell, Glasgow, 1948
Annie Reid, Glasgow, 1920s
Peter Rennie, Leith, 1928
Andrew Rigby Grey, Glasgow, 1940

Pat Rogan, Edinburgh, 1919
Cecilia Russell, Glasgow, 1898
Nettie S., Glasgow, 1930
Norma S., Glasgow, 1930
May Shields, Glasgow, 1930s
John Sinclair, Edinburgh, 1916
Annie Small, Glasgow, 1918
Bet Small, Edinburgh, 1920
Elizabeth Smith, Glasgow, 1918
Walter Smith, Leith, 1907
Val Smith, Edinburgh, 1923
Sandra Speedie, Glasgow
Stella Stewart, Edinburgh, 1919
Bette Stivens, Edinburgh, 1917
Nancy Strathie, Leith, c1921
Nan Sutherland, Edinburgh, 1913
George Telfer, Glasgow, 1920
Margaret Thomson, Glasgow, c.1950
William Thomson, Leith, 1901
Elsie Tierney, Newhaven, 1919
Mary Tolbain, Edinburgh, 1900
Christina Turnbull, Leith, 1905
John Watt, Leith, 1918
Jan Well, Glasgow, 1950s
Mrs Welsh, Leith, 1925
Ella Williamson, Edinburgh, 1916
Joan Williamson, Edinburgh, 1924
Mrs Williamson, Leith, 1908
Isa Wilson, Newhaven, 1919
Jenny Wilson, Leith, 1916
Dr Libby Wilson, Glasgow, 1920
Olivia Wilson, Leith, 1910

Foreword

When I was asked to write a foreword for this book I had honestly no hesitation in doing so. A relatively recent history of the lives of women in Scotland simply struck me as a great idea. 'She was aye workin' ' also hit home, in that my own daughters will probably use that phrase about me!

As I sit and write this I am interrupted by kids demanding 'juice and crisps', a teenager moaning because I am on the computer, the dog chewing a pair of trainers. I have to make the tea, hang up a washing, speak to my manager, contract a writer for a television show, do an interview with a journalist, try to make a charity board meeting and get out to see a pal in his show in the theatre! Yeah, she was aye workin' indeed! But what goes on in my life mirrors what most women are trying to do in a day. We deal with the minutiae of life, the stuff that gets very little notice on the 10 o'clock news, but it's all the stuff that keeps the world turning.

The history that we have been taught at school, in books, on radio and television is not the history of the everyday, and that for me is very sad. The real history of the way we have lived has disappeared and it is very distressing to feel that what women have contributed throughout their lives has been largely ignored by conventional history. Yes we know about kings and battles and plagues and fires, but we know so little about how our ancestors really lived – especially the women. Their lives were seen as not mattering as much as men's lives and what went on each day seemed trivial and meaningless. All this means that as girls and women we start to believe that our existence and our lives mean less and also that we are invisible. We fail to see ourselves reflected back in the world, which makes any woman who wants to go out in the world and be different feel like a pioneer.

It saddens me every time I go into Princes Square in Glasgow and go up the escalator to the top floor. On the way up there are beautiful drawings and paintings of the city fathers, the men who supposedly built the city of Glasgow over the centuries. There is not one woman's face there. At the time of installation there was much

2. A group of women outside a Glasgow tenement, c.1950.

argument about putting in a woman but it was decided that there was 'no woman worthy of inclusion'. How sad is that? I do not honestly believe that this city or this country has survived or flourished simply on the battles and achievements of men. Women were always there alongside and 'they were aye workin' too'.

This book goes a long way in documenting and celebrating the lives and history of Scottish women. If we know our past we can build on it and flourish thereby. Our children and our grandchildren will thank us for this as they grow and understand the hard, tough, loving and sometimes joyous lives that women had, and realise just how much of a contribution the women who went before them made.

Elaine C. Smith

Introduction

Oh she died of a whole complication of things ... She died of overwork as so many women did. The women of the working class in those days were first up in the morning and the last to go to bed. They kept the houses clean and they kept themselves clean, they kept the family's clothes clean in the worst possible conditions. They had a communal wash house in the back court with a coal fire boiler and they had to wash for the family in that. They had no equipment at all, there was no washing machines, there wasn't even hot water, you had to put on a kettle. *(Councillor Davidson, born in Cowcaddens, Glasgow in 1909, paying tribute to his mother and all the women like her.)*

This book is about the women of the tenements in both Edinburgh and Glasgow, as told by the women themselves, together with the sons, brothers, fathers and husbands who understood the burden of care that was a woman's lot.

These are personal accounts of personal experience. They show women managing relationships with menfolk, family and their ever-present neighbours, and above all trying to endure the dramas and routine of everyday life with good humour and resilience.

The tenements for these women were their childhood playground, their courting territory, the place where they married, gave birth and raised families, where they cared for elderly relatives, and themselves faced old age and death. They lived in small houses in cramped and sometimes unsanitary conditions, labouring to keep their families fed and their houses clean, and often struggling to make ends meet. They enjoyed nights at the dancing and days out at the seaside and tried to make the best of their lives. The women's stories, which include heartbreaking tales of poverty, domestic abuse, and loss, challenge many rosier pictures of such communities. This is an unvarnished view of tenement life as it was lived and remembered.

Although Edinburgh and Glasgow often see themselves as rivals and tend to deal in differences rather than highlighting similarities, the lives of most of the women who feature in this book show a surprising consistency in both cities. It emerges that the experience of living in a tenement in either Edinburgh or Glasgow in the first half of the last century varied only according to the level of poverty and attendant brutality, which was not really dependent on place.

It is easier to see a difference between the lives of respectable working-class women, governed by social mores and church authority, and of those women who flouted the strict rules of behaviour imposed on, and and indeed often perpetuated by, working-class women. These constraints held true in both cities – issues of whether women went into pubs or could drink at all, the boundaries of courtship, and sexual propriety. Respectability was determined by cleanliness and the state of your washing on the line in both cities, and common too was censure and exclusion by the women's community for overstepping the boundaries.

THE TENEMENT HOUSE

The tenement is a form of housing common to Edinburgh and Glasgow. It is a building made up of several storeys (flats), with apartments (houses) on each storey, accessed by a common stair. The tenement is found in all areas of both cities and was built to accommodate a wide range of social classes. Behind a stone facade a house might be a spacious apartment of six or seven elegant rooms or a cramped single end (a one-room house). It is the small houses of one or two rooms in which the majority of the urban population lived that concern us here.

In Edinburgh there was a high proportion of older properties in the Old Town and, more surprisingly, some elegant Georgian houses in the New Town, originally of several rooms, which had been 'made down' or subdivided into individual houses of one room. Many of these were demolished in the city's slum clearance programme during the first half of the twentieth century.

In the industrial areas of both cities in the nineteenth century thousands of tenements were constructed with an arrangement of one-room single ends and two-room room-and-kitchens on each floor. By the end of the century, some of these were built with toilets, often on the half landing. In Glasgow, more than in Edinburgh, tenements often had wash houses built in the back court, although drying greens were found behind the building in both cities.

This was the housing for the majority of the population. In 1911 66% of the houses in Glasgow and 41% of those in Edinburgh consisted of only one or two rooms.[1] As a result of housing improvements throughout the twentieth century these figures fell, but by 1951 in Glasgow half the houses still only had one or two rooms.[2]

Mothers managed to bring up large families in these confined spaces and on very little money. Families often lived close to each other and neighbours on the stair usually had their house doors unlocked. In Glasgow the walls of the entrance lobby (close) and stair were often lined to shoulder height in colourful tiles, and known as 'wally closes'. These tended not to have a door, and were open to the elements. In Edinburgh the door to the common stair was usually closed and sometimes locked, and very few had wally tiles.

People remember the gloom when entering the stair of a tenement. Pat Rogan was a local councillor for the Holyrood area of Edinburgh in the early 1960s: 'Most of the properties were in darkness and there was very little daylight brought in. ... Gas lighting would be provided on the main stairway, but off that main stairway into all these adjoining lobbies, they were all in darkness. Most of the inhabitants found their way in by touch. They learned to grope in the darkness and find their own door.' These passages were also condemned by the authorities for their lack of ventilation.

A single end could open off the shared lobby, and a room-and-kitchen house had an internal lobby with doors off to the kitchen, 'the room', a press (cupboard), and a WC, if there was one.

The kitchen was the heart of the home and in a single end it was the only room. It was the main living and eating space, and was also used for sleeping. The layout of the kitchen was remarkably standard, and similar in both cities. On the same wall as the door was the 'hole-in-the-wall' bed in its recess (now often advertised as a dining area by estate agents). This was a high bed raised up on blocks or wall battens to allow storage below – for a kist (chest), a tin bath or a hurley bed on wheels, which could be pulled out at night. There were usually feather or straw ('donkey's breakfast') mattresses, and curtains across the front, affording some privacy at

1. *Royal Commission Report* 1917, §728 p.104.
2. T. C. Smout, 'Scotland 1850-1950', in *The Cambridge Social History of Britain*.

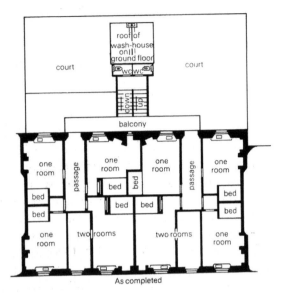

3. Plan of 21 Middleton Place, Glasgow, after improvement to add a toilet stack to the back of the tenement.

night and during the day hiding all the bedding for the other beds that was piled there.

The sink was usually against the wall opposite the bed, under the window, with one cold tap. In Edinburgh the coalbunker was built in next to the sink. It had a wooden cover that could be used as a worktop. A press was usually situated on one side of the sink. In Glasgow the bunker was built onto the side wall along with a food press and pot press, a set of drawers and two long shelves above. The bunker had a hinged lid and held two hundredweight of coal. In Edinburgh there were often a sideboard and shelves on this wall. On the side wall opposite was the fire – a cast-iron range with a large surround and mantleshelf. Some ranges had a built-in compartment for heating water, otherwise water had to be boiled in big cast-iron kettles and pots. All kitchens had a pulley for drying clothes, fixed in the ceiling above the fire. Clothes were also dried on a string stretched under the mantleshelf.

In the centre of the floor stood the scrubbed pine table and chairs. An armchair by the fire was reserved for father, with maybe a smaller one for mother. The fender sometimes had corner boxes, used for storing tools and newspaper, but also providing additional seating.

In the early years of the century most houses were lit with gas, usually a mantle on the wall above the fire. Often a gas ring was installed to the side of the fire, with a gas meter and a pile of ready pennies. Many houses were converted to electricity between the wars or after the Second World War.

The shelves were decorated with strips of cut paper or crocheted cotton and were used to store cooking equipment, crockery or ornaments. The kitchen was usually a cheerful place with coloured linoleum and clootie (rag) rugs on the floor. Photographs, portraits and embroidered and fretwork pictures might decorate the walls.

The room of a room-and-kitchen was normally used as a sleeping area. It usually had a rarely-lit coal fire and a cupboard and was sometimes used as a parlour for entertaining visitors. In some houses it was let to a lodger, while the family all lived in the kitchen.

A usual pattern was for the parents to sleep in the bed recess in the kitchen. Other members of the family could sleep on made-up beds and mattresses on the floor. If the family lived in a room-and-kitchen, the room was usually a bedroom for the children. In the room there was often a bed-closet with a bed in a large cupboard behind a closed door. This space was usually unventilated and was a constant cause of concern to the authorities. Glasgow Building Regulations of 1900 specified that 'No dwelling shall contain an enclosed bed or a bed recess which is not open in front for three quarters of its length and from floor to ceiling'. An Act of Parliament in 1913 outlawed the building of houses with enclosed beds altogether. It was however impossible to inspect and regulate existing buildings and some of these 'cubicles of consumption'[3] continued to be used throughout the century.

The shortage of space would be most profoundly felt when trying to manage the sleeping arrangements. There was a huge variety of solutions to the problem of where all the members of the family would sleep. Given such overcrowding bed sharing was an inevitable part of family life. Although there were strict taboos to regulate privacy, the authorities feared that in these circumstances incest was inevitable.

3. *Royal Commission Report* 1917, evidence of Edinburgh Burgh Engineer, Adam Horsburgh Campbell p.727.

4. Sanitary facilities were improved thoughout the first half of the twentieth century. However this photo showing a woman filling a kettle from an outside sink in central Edinburgh was taken in 1959.

In the evidence given to the Royal Commission on Housing of 1913-15 the severe shortage of a water supply was highlighted. A far higher proportion of one-room houses in Edinburgh – 43% as against 3% in Glasgow – shared a common sink.[4] The reason for this may have been the greater number of 'made down' older properties in Edinburgh, compared to the newer industrial tenements in Glasgow. There were still houses in Edinburgh where women had to collect water from outside taps well into the 1960s.

The sharing of toilet facilities was commonplace in both cities. The Royal Commission on Housing reported in 1917 that of one-room houses 94% in Edinburgh and 93% in Glasgow had no WC. In relation to two-roomed houses this figure went down, but in Edinburgh 40% and in Glasgow a significant 62% had no separate WC.[5] Toilet stacks at the back of tenements date from the passing

4. *Royal Commission Report* 1917, §571, p.77.

of the 1892 Burgh Police Act, which made internal sanitation compulsory, and were intended to replace the dry closet and privy in the back court. The WC or 'cludgie' was usually placed on the half landing and was shared by families on two floors. However outdoor toilets could be found in both cities thoughout the first half of the century.

Ella McMillan of Glasgow remembers tenement life with no facilities and the wonderful new standard of living that rehousing seemed to offer: 'You had nothing. That's why my mother fought so hard to get a Corporation house with a bathroom. That was like gold, like getting a lump of gold.'

THE SOURCES

The memories in this book are drawn from the oral history archives of Edinburgh and Glasgow Museums, which offer a rich source of material on women's lives in the first half of the twentieth century. They span the years from 1900 to the early 1960s.

In Edinburgh a joint project with the WEA (Workers' Educational Association) called *Memories and Things* was set up in 1986. The aim was to use objects from the Museum's collection to trigger memories and then to incorporate those memories in the People's Story Museum, which opened in 1989. Three reminiscence groups were set up in different parts of the city. Each week the members discussed a topic such as childhood memories, first jobs, going dancing, getting married, having a baby, housing, health, budgeting and customs and traditions. The sessions were recorded and transcribed and the transcripts given back to the participants to check over. In addition to the reminiscence sessions the staff carried out one-to-one oral history interviews on a wide variety of subjects.

Leith and Newhaven are now part of North Edinburgh, but have always had separate identities. Leith was amalgamated into Edinburgh following a referendum in 1920, much against the residents' wishes. The *Leith Lives* oral history project that ran during the 1980s produced an archive of material now stored in the Museum of Edinburgh in trust until a Leith Museum is established. When Newhaven Heritage Museum was being set up during 1993-4 a

5. *Royal Commission Report* 1917, §571-2, p.77.

community history group was brought together to develop the themes that were to appear in the museum. In partnership with Community Services Volunteers, the group met each week for reminiscence sessions. The staff of Edinburgh City Museums continue to collect oral history material relating to life in the city.

The Glasgow material was likewise collected during a variety of different projects. Interviews were carried out for the exhibition *From Here to Maternity* which opened in the People's Palace Museum in 1993. Interviews and reminiscence sessions were also set up to collect material leading up to the redisplay of the People's Palace for its centenary in 1998. The Open Museum ran a project called *1000 Glasgow Lives*. Interviews recorded in the 1970s for the People's Palace have also been included. Glasgow continues to collect oral history today drawn from the diverse communities of the modern city.

Transferring the vitality and colour of the spoken word to the page is always problematic. Some transcribers have used a spelling which reflects the sounds of dialect usage, others have used more standard English. We have not attempted to standardise these spellings.

The people who feature in this book were nearly all born during the first half of the last century. Some were in their eighties when the recording was made and are sadly no longer with us. However introductions to the quotes use the present tense throughout to retain the immediacy of the words as they were spoken. Where possible we have given the contributor's full name, but in some cases, especially on sensitive issues, a level of anonymity has been observed. These women have shown remarkable openness when talking about intimate issues. A list of contributors, with dates of birth where known and their associated town appears on pp.9-10.

We hope that the value of oral history in capturing aspects of life inaccessible to other forms of historical enquiry will be clear from the pages which follow. We thank all those who have contributed to this insight into what the women of the tenements achieved in their lives.

1

Growing Up

Nine o' us in the room and kitchen. Well ...
all the lassies slept in one bed and the laddies
slept in the other bed.

While children of the middle and upper classes growing up in the first half of the twentieth century had a more protected and prolonged childhood than is common today, their working-class contemporaries often had to grow up all too quickly. Girls especially were expected from an early age to help in the home and were often forcibly made aware of the harshness of life at a time when their own minds and bodies were still developing.

Growing up in the tenements entailed living very close to other members of the family, with little privacy or personal space. Families were often large and many people have memories of bed sharing – an inevitable and natural part of life in small spaces – and of mothers' contrivances to preserve 'decency'. Despite this proximity the onset of puberty was surrounded by reticence and few girls were helped to understand what was happening to them as their bodies developed.

Frances Milligan's recollection of crowded living conditions is typical. She was born in 1908 in Newhaven. We had a room and kitchen and a toilet outside between two families. The kitchen had a bed in the recess and underneath the bed we used to keep a big tin bath with all our coal in it for our fire. The bunker didnae really hold very much. We always had two or sometimes three beds and a chest of drawers and that was all because there was so many in the house. I was the fourteenth child. There were five or six of us in the house when I was a wee tot.

Living like this was impossible without discipline and co-operation. Joan Williamson believes that this was a valuable legacy of her upbringing. Aye, there was big families that used to stay in single ends. My sister and I shared. That was the beauty of staying in rooms-and-kitchens, you learnt to share and you do that all your life.

BED SHARING

For a large family, finding somewhere for everyone to sleep was a problem. Furniture often had to be rearranged at bedtime and there was little room to move with all the mattresses on the floor, as Molly M. of Glasgow graphically describes. I went about with a lassie I worked with who lived in a single end, and she stayed in Dalmarnock. I went up a few times with her – she had to get the younger ones ready for bed. The mattress was stacked against the wall, the table was pushed right against the sink, and this mattress was round here, and the other mattress was put down there and you had actually to jump over to get over it. You couldn't even get to the sink if you wanted a drink of water. They had to fill up whatever it was so the weans could get a drink. I have never saw anything like this in my life and yet we were overcrowded in a room-and-kitchen in Dale Street. There were a lot of wee sisters: they must have been about eight, and the father himself, nine, in that wee single end. It was just choc-a-bloc and the weans were all piled into this bed.

Betty Hepburn remembers the common practice of putting babies in drawers to sleep: A house I went to, they had twelve in their family. They used to empty the stuff in the corner out of the drawers and the drawers made three cots. *Elsie Tierney likewise recalls:* When Catherine was born she was put in the drawer because there was another baby in the cot.

Parents usually occupied the bed in the kitchen recess. Some however, like Dodo Keenan's, did not sleep together: this may have been to avoid further pregnancies. Ma father always slept in a single bed, an' ma sister an' I slept with ma mother in the double bed in the recess, an' ma brother used tae sleep through in the one room. We never called it a bedroom we only called it the room.

It was sometimes more convenient to put the children to bed earlier in the recess and then to put out extra beds for the parents. Sandra Speedie's uncle lived with them. He had the room to himself and my mother and father and my sister and myself all had to sleep in the kitchen. So my sister and I had the 'hole-in-the-wall' bed and my mother and father had one of these bed cabinets. It just looked like a piece of furniture and you just opened down the wooden bed and the mattress came out and you had to put this up during the day.

Elsie Tierney remembers the common top-to-tail arrangement at her cousins' house: I stayed at my Auntie's once, she had ten in the family. The boys were all at the top and the girls were at the bottom. You didn't have a goonie or pyjamas, just your vest and pants. You just got up and dressed yourself, there was no embarrassment.

Children often slept in the room of a room-and-kitchen, which could be cold, despite having a fireplace, as Joan Williamson points out: It was only lit on high days and holidays. You stayed in the kitchen until it was time for bed and then you had stone piggies [hot water bottles] to put in the bed. But you didn't need much, you had each other. If you had four in the bed you soon got warm.

When it came to sleeping arrangements, most parents made an attempt to separate girls from boys. Helen Nickerson grew up in a room-and-kitchen in Leith: Nine o' us. Nine o' us in the room-and-kitchen. Well, Jenny and Aggie and Betty, all the lassies, slept in one bed, and the laddies slept in the other bed. The oldest one he slept in a sort of a closet – a press. And that's where we a' slept. And my mother and father slept in the kitchen in the recess.

Molly M. recalls her father's attempts to give her some privacy. As I got a wee bit older my mum bought two double cabinet beds, one went into the kitchen and one in the room. We had an inset bed in the kitchen. The cabinet bed was for my mum and dad and I got one to me because I was the only lassie. My dad put a hook there and a hook there and a big sheet to section me off from the boys, because that was the best he could do.

Many girls like Joan Williamson went from sharing a bed with their sister to sharing with their husband. We had four girls in a bed, two at the top and two at the bottom. The three boys had shakedowns just like a camp bed, but they were older than we were. They were coming up to leaving home. I never had a bed to masel' until I lay in the hospital having my daughter. That was the first time. And then I couldnae sleep!

Occasionally children from overcrowded homes would go to live permanently with other relatives. May Shields of Pollock in Glasgow went to stay with her granny when her mother was having another baby. When my mother came out of hospital I never went back to stay. I lived with my grandmother until I was married because my grandmother had more room. She took me until my sister was older

but I was so settled with my gran I stayed there. My grandmother
was my mother.

KEEPING CLEAN

*The cleanliness of the children was an outward sign of a family's re-
spectability and was maintained by mothers with fierce effort. Much of
this was focussed on the battle against head lice, which were endemic in
tenement life, but carried a stigma. Isa Keith recalls her mother's extreme measures:* She used tae make us every night whenwe went tae
bed, we had tae comb our hair wi' a bone comb, because there was
a lot o' lousy heads about. We used tae have tae put paraffin. I used
tae hate having it on ma hair because we went intae school and
everyone could smell that you'd paraffin. I used tae say to ma mother
'I dinnae want tae have that on ma hair, everybody can smell paraffin'. She used tae say 'See, I don't like it and neither does the
beasts' – we used tae call them beasts – 'Neither do the beasts,
they'll no come on your hair when you got that'. ... And every
weekend on a Saturday she used tae put this coconut oil, it was
quite sweet-smelling. It was nice, I quite liked that, and she used tae
rub it into our hair, ken.

*Keeping clean was often an uncomfortable experience as bathrooms
were almost unheard of in the old tenements. Water for washing may
have been heated on the fire, but not always, as Molly M. recalls.* It was
cold water we had – there was no hot water. It was a black sink,
with a jaw box they called it, and every night there was no hot
water, she made us stand in the sink and she washed us all or I got
washed myself, but I just stood in the sink and when I came out my
legs were all red blotches with cold water. We were just gleaming
all over with the soap and water. It was carbolic soap. We used to
buy it and they cut it and you'd buy it like that. She made sure we
were all clean.

*Mrs Inglis grew up in Leith and remembers the tin bath, which could
be put in front of the fire:* Some of them, when the children were
very small, they used to bath them in the tub at the window, you
know. But mother had the tin bath for us. And it was wonderful
how neat it could be kept, you know. After everybody was washed
and the thing was all washed and dried out and everything was put

away – it's amazing how they could do it and still keep the place nice and tidy, you know.

Baths might be on a regular night during the week, often with the same bath water for all the children. Privacy was achieved through various rituals. Betty Hepburn describes how her mother organised things when the children got older (the 'lantern lights' were the magic lantern shows put on by organisations like the Band of Hope, on such themes as the dangers of drink). I was an only child, but my cousins stayed with us because their dad was killed in the war, so their mother went out to work during the week. So there were five of us and my mother used to say 'Lantern lights are on tonight, there's your

5. A child washing in a sink added to the outside of an old tenement block in Sandport Street, Leith, 1926.

6. Joslyn Hepburn aged three having a bath in the kitchen of Stewart Terrace, Gorgie, Edinburgh, 1955. In houses with no bathroom the bath in front of the fire was routine.

penny and away you go', and the girls all had a scrub. The boys got their wash when we went to the Brownies.

Elsie Tierney remembers makeshift privacy. If you had a wash you'd be standing in a basin in front of the fire when your brother was out, and if he was in your mother's back was always like that, hiding you. *Margaret Thomson's father would go out when she and her sister washed – unless she went out herself to the baths:* When you were getting washed in the room-and-kitchen, obviously my dad had to go out, but once a week we went to the baths and had a hot bath.

Most areas of both cities had public baths provided by the local authorities. Greta Connor remembers the different services available. You often used the baths. Nine pence, a shilling, or one-and-six [1s 6d]. Nine pence, the woman put the water in for you, about three inches. A shilling you got to put the water in yersel', and for one-and-six it was a classy place, I think you had a shower in there. That's way after the war. *Although you had more privacy in the public baths, it was not always uninterrupted, as Dodo Keenan remembers of the baths in Leith.* I mind paying three pence at the Victoria Baths in the war. The woman would come and knock on the door, 'Come on, you've been long enough!'

HELPING AT HOME

All children would be treated as an extra pair of hands and would be expected to help with heavy household tasks. However just as men and women grew up with particular expectations of their role as workers, within the family girls especially were required to help in the home and care for younger siblings. Phemie Anderson's memories of her Edinburgh childhood in the 1930s are typical. Oh yes, as we grew up we had to take our turn at helping in the house. We used to have to do the dishes and maybe one day you had to take your turn in the scullery, and in these days you had to go down and scrub the floor. It was not mopping – you really went down on your hands and knees and did it. Well we didn't have a bathroom in Bangor Road, you know it was a tin bath then. There was a toilet but no bathroom. You just had to take your turn of doing different household chores and you had to look after the wee ones, that was one of your jobs.

Small jobs were allocated to children from an early age. Dodo Keenan remembers making paper tapers with newspaper, to light ma dad's pipe and to light the gas from the fire. That and cutting up newspaper for toilet paper. *Isa Keith recalls the general distribution of jobs to the children:* We used to all have our particular job that you had to do ... you cleaned the spoons and forks or you did the boots, or the shopping. You had various jobs, and to wash the dishes or whatever.

John Barnes had to pull his weight as much as his sister: My sister and I, being roughly the same age, either had to do the kitchen fireplace, which meant polishing all the steelwork on the range and blackleadin' it, and my sister would wash the floor. The next week it would be change about. She would do that an' I would do the floor. Or you cleaned the kitchen drawer and polished up your knives. Brasso was practically unknown, but it did come in eventually. But one thing about the kitchen in these days, an awful lot of brasswork used to hang on the wall above your fireplace. You had a steel fender probably underneath, which was fretted on top, and maybe a steel stool – and these had to be all burnished with a chain burnisher. It was hard work and this was another job that you had to do.

However Flora MacDonald, like many women, has no memory of her brothers helping in the home. I had six brothers and four sisters. As we got older we did more work. My brothers were treated like gentlemen – that was general. I was the second youngest, but the ones before me got a lot to do. We didn't mind; that was our life. Well, it was the done thing for girls to do all the work. Mother used to carry the red carpet for the brothers.

Alex Kellock, growing up as one of eleven children in the 1920s, does not remember ever having to do 'as much as boil an egg' as he had older sisters who did everything for him and his seven brothers, even making their beds. He left the family home for marriage and never had to do anything in the house until he was widowed in his seventies. George Hackland, however, who lived in Newhaven had one particular hated responsibility: We had a mangle – oh, it was the bane of my life ... that was after you got home from school. You used to put off going and my mother got a chair and stood on the bunker and shouted and you couldn't make out you never heard her, everyone in the village heard her! So there was no excuse in trying to be late, you were just kept longer from going out to the clubs or a meeting, you had to get that done first. If you were first in you caught the mangle.

Girls were expected to participate in household tasks without demur because they were only doing what would for many become their job either within domestic service or in the home. The harsh circumstances of daily life meant that many women were prematurely aged and relied on their children's help: girls might be kept off school to help at home, particularly on wash day. As retired Glasgow Councillor Mr Davidson, who lost his exhausted mother when he was only four, points out: Many women died young, forcing girls to grow up quickly to take on the parental role.

Mrs Bruce was one who had to take on this role of 'little mother' whilst still at school in Leith: family members would habitually come home for the midday meal and someone had to be there to get it ready. I left school at fourteen. But before then when my mother had died ma father had gone up to the headmaster and had asked – I was

7. Bette Stivens helping her mother husk raspberries at their home in Chalmers Crescent, Edinburgh in 1927.

quite good in the house and I was left to put the soup on. I got away from school at twelve o'clock. School didnae finish till twenty past twelve ... but I got away at twelve o'clock tae put the kettle on or to put the gas under the soup tae heat the soup for dinner ... Well that was until I left school, and when I left school of course I was kept in the house, tae keep the house.

Children like her were not protected from the realities of poverty in the tenements. She has a vivid memory of adding to the family troubles one day. And we had a hard time – a hard life. Ma dad only had a small wage but he kept us all together ... I used tae run the messages in the morning. Ma father used to say go and get half a dozen eggs, or go and get bread an' lentils or whatever we wanted to make soup, 'cos ma dad used to have shift on shift you see. And I was running across Junction Bridge and I tripped on the pavement and the money, the change that I had grasped in one hand and the messages in the other rolled into the water. The money rolled into the water and I was crying. I couldn't go home. I was frightened to go down. However ma dad says, 'Now if it was an accident, it was an accident, we'll make it up. Don't worry about it.'

29

'BECOMING A WOMAN'

Growing up in the tenements of Edinburgh and Glasgow meant growing up in public: people did not expect to spend much time alone. However the physical process of puberty remained a taboo subject within respectable working-class families. Developing girls would have to learn to keep themselves 'decent' which meant keeping their bodies covered and private, and their underwear out of sight of the male gaze, as Marion McIntosh recalls of growing up in the 1950s. If there were boys or men coming into the house you couldn't have your underwear hanging on the pulley. You were told to get it down even if it was your brother.

Mrs Bruce, whose mother had died when she was a small girl, remembers the arrangement which enabled her to wash separately from her brothers. We didn't get out on a Sunday because we had tae get our clothes washed and ourselves bathed on a Sunday. I used to tae go to ma aunt's that had the girls and ma brothers went to ma other aunt that had the sons. And we had to get our clothes all washed on Sunday night ready for Monday morning.

This general code of 'decency' meant that girls were little prepared for the onset of menstruation and found the attendant emotional and physical changes terrifying. Molly M. was still very young when her body began to develop: I started at eleven and a half. I got a fright. You would. You were never warned. *Bette Stivens expresses what many felt:* It was a terrifying experience. I just woke up in the middle of the night and I thought I was going to die. Then my mother said I would have this every month. I went mad!

Joan Williamson has a vivid memory of her sister's first period: I remember my sister – we were all sitting round the kitchen table. She went to the toilet and came in screaming so I think the whole of Edinburgh heard her, 'Mum, Mum, there's blood in my knickers. What is it?'

Mothers growing up in the early years of the twentieth century having lived with taboos found it hard to talk naturally to their daughters about the onset of menses and what that might mean. Other words were used instead as a code. Elsie Tierney recalls, for example: If you got pains your mother would say 'You've altered'. Nobody was to know. It was the best-kept secret. You were just told that was you a woman now – becoming a woman. *This reluctance to discuss menstruation was perhaps part of a 'conspiracy of silence' keeping girls ignorant and therefore, it was hoped, safe from the realisation that they were becoming sexually viable women. As the age when girls get their first period varies, those who left school early could be working and classified as young adults and yet still be ignorant of the facts of life. As Mabel Dawson remembered,* I was at my work when I took mine. It was terrible.

Young women were ill prepared to know what protection to use. Sanitary pads were available (and internal sanitary protection was first marketed in the 1920s) but they were expensive – posh when you bought them with loops on the end, *according to Betty Hepburn – and women generally had to make their own from rags and cotton wool. Helen Dunbar recalls that she was given her own bag of rags:* they were used and washed each month. *Joan Williamson, born in 1924, remembers:* You didn't get the education that you get now. When you got your periods you thought something had happened to you and you got handed two pieces of cloth and some tape to put on. When it gets full you had to wash it out and make sure your brothers or sisters weren't about when you were doing this. That was your sex education. My mother had this big roll of cotton wool and would swell it in front of the fire. She would put it between a piece of sheet and fold it up and this would be pinned to your vest. She made it that big it was like a nappy. They were burned on the fire, the cotton wool. The sheet was washed – put in a pail to soak.

Joan also remembers being mystified by what she was sent to buy for her teacher: I remember I was at a Tollcross School [in Edinburgh] and the teacher used to get me to go messages to the shops across the road sometimes. And at one time in particular she gave me this money. I remember she gave me two shillings and it was for a packet of twelve towels, and I said 'What, twelve towels for this amount of money?' And I went home to my mother: 'Miss Low sent me for a message today, Mum, and she got twelve towels for I think it was one and tuppence [1s 2d]. And she said 'Twelve towels for only one and tuppence – I must go and get some!' She thought I meant towels for drying yourself.

Elizabeth Dawn from Glasgow, born in 1900, did try to talk to her daughter. She said it was all right and she knew all about it. She was eleven. *Mary Blackie, born in 1910, was different:* I never talked to mine about it even to this day.

While many girls found it hard to discuss the changes in their bodies with their mothers, many learned the facts of life in the playground and relied on their friends' knowledge, as was the case with Joan M.: That was the embarrassing part, starting your period. I was about sixteen. I had learned through the girls at the secondary school and I had started. The girl told me what she had done so I just done the very same thing. I got bits of cloth and I was washing through my pants when my mother came into the kitchen and said, 'How long's this been going on?'

THE FACTS OF LIFE

Menstruating girls might still not know much about 'the facts of life' and might be given mysterious advice such as not to wash their hair or speak to boys during a period. Bette Stivens found her mother's words confusing. My mother said to me when I got my first period 'Don't go with the boys'. I didn't know what she meant. Did she mean don't sit next to them in the picture house?!

Isa Keith had learned where babies come from quite young, when she visited a neighbour who was lying in. My mother went to see the lady after she'd had the baby and I must have been about seven or eight years of age ... I always wanted a little brother or sister because all of my friends of my age had one and I got treated like the bairn – 'You, the bairn' – and you always felt you were o' no account, you were the bairn. So I was always wanting a little sister or brother, and I was always asking my mother, and I had quite a thing about it. I used to wonder frae where they came from and my mother used to say ... we were kept very innocent ... or maybe ignorant I should say. But she used to talk about 'new baked babies' and I used to imagine that they were made in the bakeries and I was forever watching, when the bread came in to the Co-op. We used to go to the Co-op for the bakers and I used to watch these loaves to see if there were any babies I could get on the boards of loaves ...

And so when she sent me in to see this lady who'd had the baby ... she was all lying in bed with the baby feeding. I had cats. I had kittens just about the same time and we'd watched the cat and we knew where the kittens were because we used to see them moving, and I said to her, I must have been dead keen, I said, 'Where did you get that bairn?' you see, and she says 'Eh?' I asked her 'Where do they come frae?', you know, 'where do babies come frae?' And she says, 'Well you know', she says, 'where the kittens were in the cat?' And you know I never asked her anymore questions, I could accept that. I realised then, well that must be it ... She said it in such a nice sort of way you know. It didn't make me question it anymore ... It was quite settled to me. And the baby was called after my mother.

However for many like Betty Hepburn ignorance of the birth process continued through teenage years. I would say right up to fifteen or sixteen I still couldn't make out how a baby could be born. It was still in my mind that you had to get cut open. Teachers wouldn't tell you – they would have got the sack if they did.

Yet Helen Dunbar, who worked as a midwife in Edinburgh and Glasgow during the 1960s, believed that girls who had grown up during the first half of the century were better equipped for the role of parent because they had been around birth and parenting within the extended families of tenement life. The lassies I delivered in the early 1960s, they knew what to do with babies. They were from big families and as soon as they were old enough to sit in a chair they nursed the next one that came along. They looked after their sister's children or their auntie's children. There was support all round, not like it is now where the mothers are isolated.

Large families and crowded living conditions could make learning about sex a natural part of life, as it was for Mary Holligan. My mother never discussed married life or sex as it is known by now. As I was never far from the door, I never was curious. *But others like Elsie Tierney 'weren't really aware of sex', despite living in such close proximity to their parents.*

Parental control often took the place of hard information, as for this Glasgow woman: When you got to be fifteen or sixteen years old your mother would say, 'Be careful what you do, because so and so's going to have to get married.' But she'd never say why. We didn't stray because we didn't know how. We came into the house at 9 o'clock at night and you got belted if you were any later than that. *Another Glasgow woman who grew up in the early 1950s puts it bluntly:* If we had strayed like the young girls now at sixteen then you got a bashing. *Keeping girls at home could be viewed as a way of attempting to control their behaviour, or at least keep them safe.*

Anything that might signal sexual maturity, such as make-up, was firmly restricted. Isa Keith recalls an incident when she was young when she unwittingly offended her mother. I remember ma mother was going to take me and buy me shoes and she got me all scrubbed from head to foot and dressed up and all ready and she let me go outside for a minute ... there were these two girls up the stair, they were what you know the term was 'flapper' because they wore dancers' dresses. They took me up the stair tae their house and they sat me on the bunk and they did me up with curlers and waved my hair and put powder on me ... Ma ma was absolutely furious! She scrubbed me from head to foot and she never went out for the shoes that day.

Boys were not necessarily given any more information about the facts of life than girls. Mr Forbes, growing up in Leith between the wars, found out everything he needed to know from his friends. Everybody kent everybody's business, ken. So I just learned it off the rest off the laddies. But I learned young, I ken that! As soon as I kent what a lassie was, I was away! *Councillor Davidson on the other hand, growing up in an all male household in Glasgow in the 1920s, had little contact with or understanding of girls.* Females to me were much more stranger than dogs or horses because I could go and pat them or speak to them but women – oh I don't know. They were just completely strange animals.

Becoming a woman was a stage on the way to becoming a wife and mother. Flora Lindsay remembers that she might have liked to stay a child for longer: I remember saying 'I don't want it'!

2

Out of the House

When you say you lived in a room-and-kitchen, your mum
and dad lived in a room-and-kitchen, but you played out
in the street, summer and winter.

*Children spent a great deal of time out of the house: in a physical sense
the home extended out onto the stair, the back green or back court, and
the street. While girls' expectations in life were focussed upon the home,
childhood was also a time to experience something of the world outside.
Alongside play and fun were the demands of school and then work.*

*Girls often had to juggle their school studies with home commitments,
and parents could rarely afford to let them stay on at school past the
minimum leaving age. What with training for family responsibilities and
starting work, girls were not allowed the freedom of childhood for very
long.*

8. Children out in the street, Cables Wynd, Leith, 1924.

9. Girls playing 'house' in a Partick back court, c.1950. The boys are playing separately.

GAMES AND CLUBS

Girls spent hours outside where mothers could keep an occasional eye on them. The recollections of Molly M. of spending time with her friends in Bridgeton, Glasgow, are typical. We used to play out in the street, rounders, tig, ball, ropes, and when we got a bit older it was postman's knock round the backs. ... You know, playing at wee shops, going over to their back and have concerts in the back and the street entertainers coming round, the sand dancers and the tap dancers and all of us sitting on the pavement and them in the whole street to theirself shuffling up and down doing the sand dance and all that.

Unlike their brothers girls were often not free to play as they liked but had to mind their younger siblings. As Phemie Anderson says: If you went out to play, you always had a wee brother or sister with you, and you had to watch them. *For Molly M., taking the current baby out of the house so that her mother could get on was her main task.* I didn't have to help my mother in the house, but I had to watch, see

36

I was the second oldest, so I had to watch the younger ones, and each pram was brought out whenever another one was born and painted a different colour. It was big wheels. One wean it would be maybe a yellow, the next one it may be green, green's the one that sticks in my mind. It was emerald green, you know and it was a big wide pram and I had to watch the wean up and down the street while my mother done the work, done the washing out the back. Coming from school I had to watch the wean, so I was always watching weans.

Before the days of traffic, and in communities where everyone knew each other there was no fear about children playing in the streets. While boys' games tended to be more active, emphasising dares and adventure, girls' games often explored in play aspects of the marriage they looked forward to as their goal, as this Edinburgh woman recalls: Skipping games were popular, especially the fortune-telling one that predicted the name of your future husband, how many children you'd have and so on.

There was a rich repertory of singing games, many of which en-shrined common romantic aspirations:

> There stands a lady on the mountain,
> Who she is I do not know,
> All she wants is gold and silver,
> All she wants is a nice young man.

Others took an ironic look at the adult life towards which they were headed, like this rhyme collected in Edinburgh for The Singing Street.

> One shouts Mammy, give me a piece an' jam
> The other shouts Daddy, put me in the pram
> Oh, it's a life, a weary weary life
> It's better to be single than to be a married wife.
>
> When I was single I used to go and dance
> Now I am married I cannae get the chance
> Oh, it's a life, a weary weary life
> It's better to be single than to be a married wife.

Elsie Tierney remembers kissing games: Then there was Postman's Knock. 'How many stamps?' If you said six it was six kisses you got.

Skipping was very popular with girls. Mrs Inglis of Edinburgh has happy memories of mothers joining in the skipping, and of the entertain-

ments that children used to put on. One thing we used to do – and our mothers used to join us – was a long skipping rope out in the street. Our mothers used to come down and join the skipping at night. And sometimes we had wee shows of our own on the back green, you know. Somebody could sing and somebody could dance. Some couldnae sing but they had a go at it. Och, we had quite good entertainment.

When holidays and treats were so scarce, special days were a welcome focus. Dodo Keenan recalls: We always had our bonfires on Victoria Day [24th May] – it was only since the war we started having Guy Fawkes Day up here.

Hallowe'en was a good excuse for dressing up. As Betty Hepburn says, You always had a tumshee at Hallowe'en. *David Anderson tells of going guising at New Year:* We had great fun dressing up, didn't matter what you put on. You went guising and got sweeties and fruit – not money. You'd to do a wee song.

Betty Hepburn grew up in a tenement in the Gorgie area of Edinburgh in the 1920s: You were never in anyway. When you say you lived in a room-and-kitchen, your mum and dad lived in a room-and-kitchen, but you played out in the street, summer and winter, you didn't come in till bedtime. And you had your clubs and the Band of Hope. Your father would be at his work or at the pub.

The Independent Band of Hope was one of the most popular youth organisations. The meetings were attended by many children in both cities. Joan Williamson remembers: There were lantern slides at the Band of Hope and every week you got the chance go up and do a party piece and every year there was a soirée. It was a way o' life for children in these days, everybody went.

Many church and charitable organisations existed to try to counteract the perceived effects of poverty and poor upbringing in the tenements – to vary children's experience and to inculcate specifically Christian or more generally moral behaviour. They offered somewhere safe to go and something to do, and were popular for the treats they laid on to sweeten their improving aims. The majority of children went to Sunday School, at least when they were younger, as Stanley Jamieson attests: Most people went to Sunday School. Sunday Schools then were packed out. I know lots of Sunday Schools today where there's not more than a dozen children, but Sunday Schools then were up to a hun-

10. Children at a Sunday School run by the Edinburgh Medical Missionary Society, c.1924. Most children were regular attenders at Sunday Schools: as well as religious instruction they provided treats like annual picnics.

dred children. There was far more of them. There was one at every street corner.

Ella Williamson's father, who was a member of the Labour Party and an active union man, sent his children to Socialist Sunday School instead. I suppose it was his way of teaching us socialism rather than ... him teaching us it himself. ... The highlight was if there was a new baby and they had this naming service as well. The mother and father and the baby were there and they promised to bring the child up as a socialist and we sang hymns. *Girls would often stay on longer than boys, who stopped wanting to go at about twelve. As Ella says, later they might join other socialist organisations:* When we became teenagers, there was what they called the League of Youth, say sixteen and older ... and then they got married in I suppose their twenties.

The Leith Provident Co-operative Society ran a Children's Circle which Nan Sutherland attended in the 1920s: We used to go to the Leith Circle, and we had festivals, pantomimes in the Ferry Road, choirs and country dancing, elocution lessons.

FURTHER AFIELD

The big attraction of Sunday School for children was the traditional annual picnic. These were for some their only trips out of the city, as Stanley Jamieson vividly remembers: They were really big occasions. You'd go to the church hall and you went to the church hall with a tape round your neck and a tin can hanging on it. Or if your mother felt herself a wee cut above the rest, then she took a real cup in a message bag ... But most people had a tin tied round their neck, and you had your ticket. When we were all mustered there, each teacher with their class behind them, we had a great long crocodile, maybe more than a hundred folk ... would board the train and off you went ... and away to Davidson Mains, or Juniper Green or whatever, or Balerno, and spend the whole day playing games, having lunch, having tea, running races, winning prizes, falling over, stepping in cow pats! Great!

Betty Hepburn has similar memories: There was always a party went away early and they took a lorry and all the stuff with them. all the eats, and lit the fire and got it going, so when you arrived there it was all ready. We went to Riccarton, out to Balerno, down to Davidson's Mains. One year we went to Kinghorn. If you were a member of a Sunday School you didn't have to pay anything. But if your mother or a friend wanted to come, they paid. ... We went on a hired bus with streamers and balloons. You always sang there and you always sang back.

Sometimes children's parents would give them a tram fare to take them off somewhere for a picnic; occasionally it was a proper family outing. The seaside at Portobello was popular with Edinburgh families, as Dodo Keenan remembers. We used to get tuppence and bread and margarine and a bottle of water and we'd go down to Portobello. We'd spend a penny going down by tram, but we'd spend the other penny and have to come walking back. We'd go once during the Trades, all our family. But we made a fire and brewed up tea. Then they had rowing boats ... A right big family outing. *Glasgow families also came to Portobello for their Fair holiday later in July. Betty Hepburn used to see them:* I remember we always went when it was the Glasgow Fair because the Glasgow folk always camped on the sand anywhere. We always used to go down on the Sunday.

11. Joan Fraser with her mother, sisters and brother on a day out at Cramond, Edinburgh, 1929. The swimsuits cost 6d from Woolworths.

Betty was lucky enough to have an aunt who had a holiday hut. We used to go to the Carlops. My auntie used to have one of those wooden huts at the Carlops and we used to go there and it didn't cost us anything. We used to have their kids and then our auntie came and she'd look after us. We'd buy everything we needed at the village shop and get out there in a bus. We'd go guddling in the stream and we'd fry the fish if we caught any.

She remembers also going off cycling or camping with friends when she was a little older. The only cycling I did was down to Cramond. We used to spend the weekend in a tent. There were boys and girls and we used to hire bikes from a bike shop along Dalry. The man there was awful nice and he'd see the bikes were OK. We'd dash along after our work was done and cycle away to Cramond with our half-loaf and stay in a tent overnight. We'd just pitch on the shore. You went up to the farm for your milk and eggs.

SCHOOLING

Play and outings were a welcome respite from the school, chores and jobs that occupied much of children's time outside the home. Those with ability could pursue a challenging range of academic subjects at school, and gain a School Leaving Certificate on completion of secondary education. But financial pressures forced many to drop education when they reached the minimum school leaving age, which was fourteen from 1901 until just after the Second World War.

Educating girls beyond their need was anyway considered by many parents a waste of time and an unnecessary burden, as Phemie Anderson remembers. I didn't get a leaving certificate because I left when I was fourteen, but we got exams – very much so. I took what we called a commercial course at David Kilpatrick. That consisted of all your main subjects. I had French, English, Geography, History. We did some cooking, domestic science of a sort, and typing and shorthand, art. There was a variety of subjects you had to take. I always remember when it came near to exam time, the revision you had was out of this world. You'd think you were sitting for a scholarship instead of just an ordinary half-hour exam ... I seen me going home and having arithmetic, algebra, history, geography, all revision homework to do for that. I remember one night my dad was out and I was watching my brothers and sisters – I don't know where my mother was – and I said to my mum, once they were all in bed I would do my homework. And I was on the kitchen table and had all these books spread out and my dad came in, and here's me still doing my homework, and he just took my books and closed them up and that was that. He says, 'You're doing no more', and he had to send a note to school to say that – no way – you're taking some nights two or three hours sitting at home.

While the authorities tended to overlook patchy attendance by girls, there was an inevitable tension between the needs of the home and the legal requirement to attend school. Tired and ill mothers were common, and it was the fate of many girls to become second mothers to younger siblings. Mrs Williamson of Leith was typical: And then I was supposed to stay on at school but my mother had my young brother, you see, and I had to leave school and look after him because she took ill. That's how I left school before I should have. When I was

12. A girl playing schoolmistress, with her class well under control, in a Glasgow back court, c.1960.

fifteen I left school and I should have been staying on till I was sixteen really.

As girls were likely to need housewifery skills more than academic achievements, many schools streamed children so that those not expected or able to study for academic subjects could learn domestic skills such as cooking and cleaning. Girls were essentially taught how to be house-wives, with the school resembling a home – except that mother who did everything was replaced by a teacher for each specific domestic skill.

43

Women learning the 'mysteries' of looking after home and family were still taught by other women. Agnes Boyd remembers her school in Leith: the laundry teacher and the cookery teacher and the sewing teacher. That's in your housewifery, like. We had cooking one day, and we had laundry the second day, y' know. That was like twice a week, one for laundry and one for cooking. In Cooper Street School the top flat was the laundry room.

They were taught to cook plain simple fare as Rita Flannigan remembers: The cookery lessons that you got at school were the sorts of things your mother made – toad in the hole and scones.

Girls who left school at fourteen could thereafter opt to attend evening classes, including classes in domestic skills. Mrs Bruce had this fond memory of domestic science school: When I was fourteen I joined the night school for cooking, and – cookery lessons and what else, sewing – sewing. I made one or two wee blouses and things in school. You had to buy material; I think it was about sixpence a yard in those days. Well then, this other girl and I, teacher said, 'Do you know where the potatoes are kept?' I said, 'Yes they're down in the cellar' ... another girl and I was sent; there wis no boys in our class at that date ... Well we were up at the top flat in the school and three flights of stairs to come and along a corridor and up another stair and along another corridor and up another – three flights. And we got to the top flat and of course we were giggling 'cos it was getting heavy, the bag, and we were trailing – Did the girl not let hold of the bag and the potatoes all rolled out and they rolled all round those stairs and down and down and down. Well, I could do nothing for laughing. Oh dear. We got an awful row when we went in with half a bag of potatoes instead of a bag. Well the two of us ran ... and went down and collected all the potatoes we could, in our skirts, and brought them up.

STARTING TO EARN

Both boys and girls in poor families had their career options limited by pressure to leave school and start earning as soon as possible. It was easy to understand why some children, particularly older girls, might resent their lack of opportunity. For Mary K., growing up in the 1930s, a promising career as a singer was thwarted as she was needed at home to help care for the family: her mother 'simply could not let her go'. Apart from childcare and domestic help there was the fact that she would soon be able to work in the local factory, earning 10 shillings a week, most of which would go into the family purse.

Younger children often worked before or after school to augment the family income. Meg Berrington and her brother and sister all worked as youngsters in Leith in the early 1920s. I used to deliver newspapers. The shop was down at the foot of our stair and the newspaper person was called Miss Anderson. I used to get up at six in the morning to deliver papers when I was still at school, when I was eleven. I think eleven was the minimum age in these days. Another sister went and delivered milk in the morning and my brother delivered milk, he worked with the Co-op in North Forth Street. The younger ones in the family didn't do this because some of us had started to work while the younger ones were still at school so they didn't have to do this.

Mrs Gardiner was one who became the main breadwinner in her family though still little more than a child herself. My mother and my father died young. My mother was forty-two when she died, and my father died before that, and I went to work. I was in my teens and ... I was the only one working and I had to bring my wage every week and pay the rent and look after them. Just my wages, there was no help then. In fact, if there was, I never asked for it. ... So, I had a time in bringing them up you know, but I kept them under my thumb and they were all decently married and respectable and nobody can say anything about us, so there.

Mrs Gardiner managed to provide and care for the family despite the unreliable wages she received in Duncan's, the chocolate factory in Leith. Six o' clock in the morning till six at night and in the summertime when we couldn't get to work for the chocolate, I started out at four in the morning. ... Perhaps we got to work to nine o' clock depending on the heat ... and then we got away for the rest of the day and came back at six o'clock at night to work until ten. There was very little wages in the summertime. The boss used to say, 'Well you made good wages in the wintertime, you should have saved.' But what young girls would have saved? *It was a hard struggle: long and split shifts meant that inevitably she had to leave her younger sister unsupervised in the house to get herself out to school.* She was a young girl and she used to go away and leave the gas burning all day in the house – she forgot to put it out. One time, I came home at night and the whole house, the whole o' the people in the tenement was in the house – she'd set the chimney on fire putting the fire on for me coming in at night. ... And then my brother would fight with my sister and I was always going to leave them: 'I'm going to put you in a home, I'm not going to stand it.'

Outside of wartime only certain jobs were considered suitable for females. Cecilia Russell from Glasgow was orphaned early. Her father died six weeks before she was born. When her mother died she was determined to make her own way in the world and to get a job she wanted to do, despite the disapproval of her siblings. They were frightened that something would go wrong with me: there were a lot of bad men about, just the same as there are now. In fact I was doing my pupil teacher. Oh my sister wouldnae have it! It wisnae for me at all, not at all. My sister thought I was going to work in the dairy. But God had given me brains no to humph milk carts. I was above that! I went to another sister who was married to a policeman and I said I was going to look for a job. Every day when I brought in a *Citizen* her husband would say, 'No, no, no! You can't let her out like that! You can't. Something will happen to her ... Something will happen to her'.

At fifteen years of age in 1913, Cecilia eventually found work with the Scottish United Loan Company in Garscube Road, though she encountered the normal reluctance to employ girls rather than boys. It was a Saturday and I got this paper ... So up I went and they said it was a boy they were looking for. I said, 'Please, please let me have the job, you don't know how anxious I am to have it.' It was a pawn office and the job was to paste a ticket onto the bundles – it was nothing to me. This girl Jean Donnachie – she was an awful fine woman. I said to her, 'Oh please! Do something on my behalf, because I'm a double-breasted orphan, and I need the money.' So I got the job. Up and doon these ladders! Pullin' oot the bundles! Oh I was just an expert at it.

Armed with a reference from the 'old humphy-backed councillor' that owned the company she later applied for work to the City Pawnbroking Company in Anderston. I went down and handed in this letter – it must have been a glowing report. 'Oh', he said, 'What a pity – it's

13. Young female staff at a Buttercup Dairy Company shop in Glasgow, 1930s.

really a boy we're looking for'. I said, 'Look', I said, 'I've heard this already' – this was before Women's Lib mind you! I said, 'I'll do anything for you', I said, feminine like. 'Oh well, I'll give you a trial.' Well, I started at, I think it was seven shillings a week. I got a rise every week for a month.

Cecilia had stayed with her sister but found her too strict. Her next step to independence was to pay for her own lodgings – though this took almost all her earnings. I left and went into digs – I was very brave – nine shillings a week was my wages, which I paid to the landlady. Cumlodden Drive in Maryhill to Anderston, and back again at night.

It was hard for working girls to lead an independent life – economics and even loneliness often kept them at home. Mary Holligan remembers

47

her mother had to give her own mother all her wages from J. Stuart's Cotton Mill in Musselburgh where she made nets. My mother left home to go and stay with a workmate in Musselburgh, but she was very unhappy and not having much money had to return home. She used to tell me she got sixpence for her pocket money, off which she had to keep two pence for the plate at church. She used to sneak to the Town Hall dancing which cost two pence admission, one penny for cloakroom, one penny for striped balls [sweets].

Girls were generally expected to hand over the majority of their wages to their mother as Ella Williamson recalls of her time working in a fishmonger's in the early 1930s: I got eighteen shillings when I went back to the job at Meadowbank, and I gave my mother twelve and kept myself the other six. But we managed. If I wanted to take a bit of fish home for the tea the boss never said no.

A girl needed at home to look after sick parents or siblings would have to take time off work. Chrissie Hollinsworth had to leave Crawford's in Edinburgh: Well my mother took a tired heart, and I worked in Crawford's at the time, and I was six weeks off my work looking after her. I kept the house, looked after the family, cooked the meals and after she got better I went back to work. I used to do a washing a night for her. Scrub the floor and cover it with newspaper.

The hard work of running the household was always the first priority: Mrs Bruce was eighteen before she was allowed to go out to work. I wasnae allowed to go out to out to work though, I wanted to go out to work. I wasnae allowed because I was needed in the house, because I has to do the washing and ironing and everything. I had tae do all that myself. *Working at least meant that she could bring some money into the house and have a shilling to herself to go to the pictures. Most girls growing up and waiting to be married valued the small measure of independence and taste of life outside the home that work gave them.*

3

Are Ye Dancing?

We all had to be in the house by a certain time. If you
came in late by God ye got a hammering.

*As girls left school, and usually started to work outside the home and
earn some money, they began to have a little more freedom to go out and
thus to encounter the man they would marry – for married life was
accepted as the life goal of all young women. Choices of where to go for
fun and courtship were severely limited compared with today, by money
and by social conventions.*

*Most couples met at church, at work or at the dancing, but however
they met, it was important to gain parental approval. Parents kept a
close eye on their daughters to make sure they did not stray. In small
communities everybody knew everybody in any case, and often people
might end up marrying someone they had known all their lives. If a girl
or young man developed a reputation for loose morals the whole community would soon get to know about it.*

GOING OUT

*Girls were usually only allowed out once all the jobs were finished and
under strict conditions as to when they would be back in. Going out in
town involved trips to theatres like the Gaiety in Edinburgh or the Al-
hambra Palace in Glasgow, or more commonly to the cinema or the
dancing.*

Jean Hay, born in Edinburgh in 1914, loved the shows: Every Saturday night we went to the theatre, Lyceum or Empire. 7.30, every
Saturday night. it cost you 6d for the gods. *Mrs Bruce went regularly
to the cinema in Leith and met her husband in the queue in 1923.* An'
we used tae go to the Kirkgate ... an' I met this chap in the Gaiety
queue, an' he said, 'I'll keep a seat for you'. Never mind we are at
the back of the queue; he was at the front of the queue. However
he always managed to keep a seat for ma friend an' I near the front.
So that's where I met ma husband.

14. The cinema played an important part in young people's lives: Partick Cross, Glasgow, c.1950.

In the 1920s and 30s there were many cinemas in Edinburgh, while Glasgow boasted over 120 at its peak. Molly M. worked at the Royal Cinema in Glasgow, selling ice-creams, and that is where she met her future husband. I used to stand at the back because you had snowballs and ice lollies and ice-cream and it got heavy. That is where I met my man. He used to run about with the street bookies and they stood round the corner or the back, and the pubs shut at 9.30pm and when the bookies finished they went for a pint and they used to always go into the second sitting at the Royal.

Cinema bought glamour and a little romance into the lives of ordinary working-class people. Christina Turnbull has warm memories of going out. They really were happier times and of course the girl didn't pay. I mean the girl never paid. The young man would have been absolutely insulted. My husband liked the theatre and he liked the pictures, and we would be – this was when we were a bit older – we would be there at the pictures on a Monday and the pictures on a Wednesday and the pictures on a Saturday. Definitely.

Men were expected to pay for all social activities and if they had little money women had to accept that they could not go out. This was Ella Williamson's fate. You couldn't afford to go to the pictures very often or things like that and anyway Alex worked till seven o'clock on

50

Saturday too, it was really too late to go to the pictures ... but he would say, 'I cannae afford it, to take you'. But in those days if you suggested you paying that was a no-no. Even going Dutch they wouldn't do that you know. Because he couldn't pay we just did without. You just went for walks and then at weekends, well either I would be at his parents for a meal, and he would be at my parents, because you couldn't afford to take meals outside.

Even when money was short it was the done thing to buy your girl-friend chocolates. This represented an unexpected ordeal for Mary Holligan. He wouldn't have much money by the time he'd paid his board to his sister, but every time we went out, I always got without fail a box of Terry's All Gold. They were the best in those days, but I never ate one: I was so shy then, the thought of chewing and rustling of paper made me uncomfortable. It was a long time until I could eat one. Also if we went up town or anywhere out of the district I was too shy to leave him to go to the toilet, and that is the truth.

DANCING

The dancing holds a special place in the memories of most of those who grew up during this period: it was a passion for many young people. As Bette Stivens says, If you were a teenager you wouldn't put up with the knitting. Your mother would be doing that. For you it was the dancing! *Some went very frequently, like Mary J. from Shawlands, Glasgow:* I read, but as a young girl I was at the dancing every night of the week! *The dance halls were flourishing from the 1920s until after the Second World War. Mrs Welsh of Edinburgh remembers:* It was really packed after the war when the big bands came – oh probably about seven hundred or eight hundred people.

Getting dressed up was all part of the occasion, as Olivia Wilson recalls of the late 1920s. Oh, you always got dressed up. When I was eighteen the skirts had shortened and we were wearing them to the knees but I can remember one of lace. Very shiny stockings, flesh coloured stockings, high heels. And then a little bit later if you were going anywhere you wore a full length dress, the fashions changed again. And then of course there was still balls and that was a gala rig-out. Although we were poor it was amazing how many of them we went to. There was always a Beauty Queen like

15. Annie Wallace borrowed this dress from her friend. She had her photograph taken at the Empire Studio, Edinburgh in 1925 before going dancing.

the Queen of the May. You see we had things to look forward to.

Women did not have many clothes and would wear their one good dress over and over again. Mrs Bruce remembered her 1920s dress clearly. I remember this Mary Dixon that stayed in the Kirkgate. She was making overalls: well it was a bright print material she'd got, and to make them fancy she had lace round the edges and a wee bit lace round the arm. I can still remember that dress. That was before we were married and we used to go to the dancing, and that was always my dress for the dancing. It was washed and ironed as often. I was dancing with this chap and he says to me – there was mirrors all round the hall – and he says to me, 'Excuse me, do you know your dress is hanging down?' Well, I was so offended, I didnae want to dance with him again and I says, 'That's not my underskirt its my dress.' It was the lace hanging down on my dress. That was the style. We used to make our own. You just had to make use of what you had. I still remember that chap saying that to me. I was quite fair away with myself, having a look at myself in the mirror. I thought I wis no bad looking!

Girls often made their own clothes and even jewellery, as Bet Small did around the time of the Second World War. We used to have tiny glass beads and we used to make necklaces and brooches and embroider them on your dress. We used to do that at night.

Before the advent of disco, dance halls employed big bands like Billy McGregor and the Gaybirds who played at the Barrowland in Glasgow in the 1960s. Dances were formal until quite late on: girls carried dance cards to be marked with partners for specific dances. Olivia Wilson liked that system: You had a dance card and you knew who was going to dance with you and who wasn't and who was going to get the last dance. That was good.

Many like Helen Nickerson learned to dance without any lessons. The way we learned to dance was we used to watch the fellas dancing, and it would be a ladies' choice and we used to touch the good dancers, and that's the reason we learned how to dance. We didnae pay for dancing lessons. *Good dancers had regular partners, as Madge Earl from Edinburgh, born in 1910, recalls.* I had special partners. One for the waltz, one for the tango, one for the blues, one for the quickstep, right through the night. And many's the row I've had then they said, 'Are you going up?' and I said, 'Sorry I'm booked!' They all came from up town, up the Canongate to Fairley's. My mother was a waitress there and I'd sit with her in the lounge and I got my supper.

Some women were left without partners for at least the early part of the evening, as Bette Stivens explains. A lot of chaps wouldn't come in to the dancing until after 10, after the pubs were out. Or they'd be in and stand at the back. They'd come in to watch the talent. *John McGowan, a doorman at the Barrowland in Glasgow in the 1960s, would mingle on the dance floor to encourage the women.* There were wallflowers ... We used to talk to them, obviously they have paid their money and they are entitled to enjoy themselves. So we were standing at the side dancing with them just to break the ice because they have stood for an hour there and done nothing. Whether they are ugly or beautiful it makes no difference. As we knew most of the people we used to say, 'Oh give them a turn, there's a lumber for you.'

Edinburgh women reminiscing about the old days at the dancing remember all the lines, which Betty Hepburn says came over from

Glasgow. It was nae bother getting a dance. 'Are you dancing?' 'Are you asking?' 'If you're dancing then I'm asking.' 'Well if you're asking then I'm dancing', that was the opening line.

It was considered rude to refuse to dance with a man and once dance cards were no longer used women had to be careful not to offend men or they could become aggressive, as Mrs Welsh recalls. If a chap came up to ask you to dance and you refused him you wouldnae dare go up with anybody else. I can remember there was one chap came up and asked me to dance. Oh he was drunk. I said, 'No thank you.' It was about 1 o'clock in the morning. He said 'If you go up and dance with anyone else I'm going to thump them!' and I was dreading Johnny coming back with the coats. However when Johnny came back we were going to do the last dance with our coats on ready to go you see. However when he saw the size of Johnny he never bothered. Oh. But you wouldnae dare!

Many a marriage was made in the dance halls in Edinburgh and Glasgow, but more short term encounters began there too, as for this

16. Dance cards were carried by girls who filled them out with the names of their dancing partners. This way, if another man asked them for a dance they could show they were already booked.

Glasgow woman: I met my man at the dancing but I did work with him. That is when I found out he was kicking with someone else. The lassie at the next machine asked if I knew this big guy because she was going out with him and I told her he was my man. Needless to say that did not last long.

In Edinburgh each place had its own reputation, as Betty Hepburn recalls: There was Eldorado or Hanna's Ballroom and the Palace Ballroom at the Foot of the Walk, or Stewart's Ballroom. Picardy, now that was the naughty one, and Fairley's. Your mother told you, don't go near them, but you had to to get the good dancers. *People like Olivia Wison would travel into the city for a night out.* You see the people of Leith quite liked going up town. We would say 'We're going up town, we're going to the pictures'. And of course we also went dancing, to the Marines, the Marine Gardens.

Glasgow was dancing mad between the wars and had many well-known halls, such as the Locarno and the Clarendon. Later the largest was the Barrowland, which could hold close to 2000 people. John McGowan recalls: On a Friday night a queue formed from the door of the Barrowland up the Gallowgate, up Gibson Street, along Moncur Street which is along the back of the Barras. It was like a square. This was a queue to get into the Barrowland. If a girl was looking for a boy then it was the place to go and vice versa. We used to have carnival nights. What we had was hatches under the ceiling and we used to fill them up with balloons in the loft. Billy McGregor would shout 'It's carnival time', and we had to release the balloons. For the sake of a few hundred balloons it was amazing how people changed from being grumpy to being happy, it was unbelievable. The bursting of balloons would go on for about three quarters of an hour and we never had any trouble because people were that busy bursting balloons.

However in later days trouble often did happen on the dance floors, fuelled by drink and the volatile street gangs of Glasgow in the 1950s, as Jimmy Phillips remembers: A lot of good people came into the Barrowland and a lot of bad people as well. I would say more good than bad because we had all the gangs from Bridgeton, the Gorbals and the Calton, but you got to know the ones you had to keep an eye on. But then again if you got them coming in from Maryhill it was mayhem. You had them on this side of the dance hall with two or three people dancing and then you had the other ones at the other side. As you looked you could see the flashes of knives or whatever. There were some bad times ... We used to take the drink off them as well but even taking the drink didn't work Every Monday morning, we had onion bags and used to fill twenty-seven at least of those bags with bottles.

John McGowan met his own wife at the Barrowland when he was working there. One of my friends who also became my best man when we got married introduced me to her. I used to say that I wasn't that bothered because women were ten a penny to be honest. I wasn't a bad looking boy in those days and I had a lot of patter. As soon as they came in they used to ask if they could have my carnation when I was finished. It wasn't just my carnation they were after. I used to give it to the one I was going away with when I finished. My wife used to come up and a few of my ex-es used to pull her up and tell her they were still going with me, because we went out for seven years before we got married. I mellowed out and did my job and went home. I was in love with her. I didn't need anyone else.

Billy McGregor and the Gaybirds used to play to the fact that people went there in the hope of meeting a future partner: There was a particular tune we used to call 'The Wedding' and so he dresses me as a minister. He then dresses up the female vocalist as a bride, wee Johnny was dressed up as Old Mother Riley who was meant to be the bride's mother and the male vocalist was dressed up as the groom.

COURTSHIP

Most young women went about with their future husbands for some time before they got married. In the main women met men of similar backgrounds and in similar financial circumstances, and often from the same community. Betty Laing, living in Denniston, Glasgow after the Second World War, did not have far to look to find a husband. I met him through a girl who stayed up the stairs. She was friendly with this other chap and we all stayed in one building. We didn't really start going out together until I was sixteen, we went together for about three years, were engaged for two. I had known him for seven years before we got married.

Like many women, Ella Williamson, born in 1916, married a man she became friendly with through a common interest. I met him at the Union, and then my brother worked near, in the Co-op and Alec worked in the Co-op, so that's how I got to know him. But we went about quite a while, we went to these Union meetings and come down the road, you know it wasnae a case of love at first sight or anything like that, you know, it was a gradual friendship. I make a joke and say that I always wanted to marry a tall, dark, handsome man that worked in the Co-op.

Spending time together during courtship often simply involved going on walks, as for Mary Holligan: As I always felt alone I used to go to where I thought my boyfriend was working. I used to look in a shop window that had the blinds down so I could see him across the road. We went for long walks together, and we used to sing. He taught me the words of the Mountains of Mourne and we would also sing in Latin when we were walking.

As more single women began to earn their own keep, their lives broadened and they began to take part in more mixed group events outside the home, increasing their chances of meeting a stranger. Barbara Anderson met her man when she was working in the Astley Ainslie hospital in Edinburgh in 1929. His father was a porter in the Royal Infirmary and when our porter at the Astley Ainslie was taken ill ... I was seventeen and a half, and we married when I was twenty-one.

The war years allowed men and women to mix more freely, and relationships developed quickly. Andrew Rigby Grey's father used to commute between Edinburgh and Glasgow during the First World War when he worked with Meikle. He always used to wave at the munitions girls when passing Polmont, including one with flaming red hair. One day he threw this girl a box of chocolates and a note from the train window. The next day he got off at Polmont and saw her. They married. She was twenty-five years younger. Her name was Joan Hutchison.

Mr Gibson met his wife during the Second World War. I knew her by sight. I had got myself a car at this time and I was going to take a medical at Turnhouse, and this girl, this WAAF, was waiting for transport. I said, 'I'll give you a lift'. So that was where it happened.

Alf Daniels was a Londoner. He came to visit a friend in Partick, Glasgow, and met a girl in the same tenement block. This was also Alf's first encounter with tenement life. I came up to Glasgow from the Royal Navy and my mate lived two doors down from where I lived. I went in to see this boy and they were going out. The door opened and in came this lump of haggis and I thought 'She is for me'. She was only fifteen and I was eighteen. I came up here to see her mum. I had never seen a tenement building before, it was all semi-detached houses in England. The problem when I came up here, I thought the wife's house was the whole building ... there was no answer at the door and she knew I was coming up. Eventually the door opened and this woman asked me what it was I was after, and I told her I was looking for Irene and I asked if she was in, and she told me, she wouldn't be in there as that was her cludgie. I asked her what the cludgie was and she said the shit-house. That was my first introduction to tenement buildings.

French born Lise Friedman went on holiday in Glasgow just after the Second World War. She had spent the war in hiding in France and was then living in London. A very religious woman, she was prepared to consider an arranged marriage at the other end of the country. I stayed with this family whose father was a member of the Jewish clergy and a suggestion was made that as I was here in Glasgow there was a fabulous Scotsman, Jewish and religious: of course I wasn't interested – I came for a holiday and I wasn't interested. However the idea was pursued and I met that Scotsman. He visited me in London and we became a Franco-Scottish union, with Franco-Scottish products, a son and a daughter. My heart was definitely in the marriage. In Orthodox circles we still believe there is a point in arranged marriages. When I got married I was a little more mature than the average bride, I think I was thirty-four years old. I had opportunities to marry before but first of all my priorities was to find someone who could share religious views and whose observance of Judaism would be similar to mine. I feel it is important because one hopes for children.

KEEPING SAFE

Many parents, aware that young girls were vulnerable to men and anxious to keep them away from the consequences of being seduced – illegitimate children and a sullied reputation – tried to make sure they always knew where their daughters were going and with whom. Certain places were not considered respectable.

Young women were often forbidden to drink alcohol, which was seen as a man's vice: girls under the influence were also deemed more likely to 'stray'. Molly M. from Glasgow once lost a job because her mother heard that she had been drinking at the works dance. Now that was a lie, I didn't even touch drink ... It was a works dance, and it was a Friday night and I was working on the Saturday morning, and the next thing the gaffer came round and says you better put on your coat, your mother has come out to lift your books.

Mary Holligan from Edinburgh remembers rules on where you could go: One wasn't allowed to roam aimlessly; you had to be going somewhere. I wasn't allowed to walk on the Prom [Portobello], as Mum said 'Only strumpets walked there'. But coming out of the church we decided to take the risk to walk along on the road home to be in time for Mary to catch her bus to go up town.

There were two chaps sitting on a bench. Mary recognised one of them; they had been to church too, so we were introduced to each other, but as Mary said, 'Wait till they hear we come from Newcraighall, they will be off like snow off a dyke.' But no, as we said cheerio, one of them said 'We will walk you home.' One of the chaps was very quiet spoken and I couldn't get a good look at them but as we got into more light I liked him. But as we walked Mary crossed over to walk with Dennis and I had to walk with his cousin Jimmy, but at a narrow stretch of road, Dennis crossed and came over to me. I was very pleased, I could hardly speak ... and of course it was my first date and of course the crunch came when I got home, as my mum knew the time that the church should be out, so she was standing at the door when I got near and she said, 'What's this fella? I thought you were at church. Who is this chap?' I replied he was at church with his cousin and offered to take us home. She asked his name and when he told her, he got a great welcome as she knew his mother very well. So I was happy, so we made a date to go to the pictures at Portobello.

Respectability was 'the badge of honour' in working-class communities, and in both Glasgow and Edinburgh the church had a firm hold on the moral well-being of the young people. Church hall social events, or church outings were seen as a good way for women to meet respectable

17. Two young women in their summer best: Marion Bottomley and May Lindsay on Marion's brother Charlie's Royal Enfield Motorbike. Taken in 1952 outside the balconied tenements at Dumbiedykes, Edinburgh.

men – church-goers were less likely to have vices such as drinking or gambling, and it was usually possible to find out about their background from other church members. For some who had known the devastation of two World Wars the moral code of socialism and was the answer as they strove to rebuild the world. Men who belonged to a church or to an organisation like the Independent Labour Party (ILP) were likely to be approved choices for clean-living young women. Ex-Councillor Davidson of Glasgow recalls: I ran into an organisation which was advocating an international language, Esperanto. Now remember I was brought up during the First World War and it was ordinary men who went to slaughter. I felt if there was a simple language for uneducated people like myself we could understand each other better. Anyway I took up with this language and met a girl who was similarly interested. Her name was Annie. Fifty years with the right woman.

Parents would judge harshly any man who flouted convention, even their own sons, as Mr Forbes of Leith testifies. My mother used to shout out o' the window in Lapicide Place, 'Leave these lassies alone!' I was always winchin' and runnin'. And I'd run intae a stair, and when I came intae the stair I'd get a hud o' them [makes kissing sound]. Oh! my mother used to shout out the window regular!

Christina Turnbull recalls parental attitudes: You always brought the boy or girl home first of all, you know. Kept your fingers crossed. But if you were late in getting home, I know my mother and I suppose most mothers would be the same – 'Well he doesn't think very much of you if he keeps you out till this time on a Sunday night.' And that would be all that was said. No, eh, 'What does he do?' or anything like that. I suppose they would get that bit by bit out of you.

Men were expected to look after women morally, financially and physically. The girl had to be taken home and this could mean a long walk for the man very late at night. One Edinburgh man courting in the 1940s recalls: As you got older ye went to the dancing and that. If it was a late night dance which was normally one o'clock ye could maybe walk a girl home and get yourself home. Ye never thought of anybody going to mug you.

Helen Nickerson's parents were very strict with her and her sisters about deadlines for coming home from the dancing. She [mother] used to let you go to the dancing. Aggie, Jenny and I. And we darenae come in one at a time. When the three of us went out the gither, we used to come back the gither. It was a shilling to get in and a penny for your bus or your tramcar. You either took the tramcar going and hoping that they got a boyfriend, a lift hame. But if you werenae sure that you were going to get a pick up, as they used to cry it, we used to have to walk hame. So we had to run hame 'cos we all had to be in the house by a certain time. If you came in late by God ye got a hammering and you were getting kept in the following week.

If they got a boyfriend I used to stand in the corner. I never believed in taking pals hame. I was always that strict about myself because I always said they were after one thing. Jenny and Aggie had boyfriends and I used to stand in the corner and wait until they had finished their snogging and we all went in together. I'll tell you one night we werenae. Jenny went on a fella's motorbike and my

mother had bought us all new raincoats and Jenny's was a white
one and Aggie's and I a sort of beige. Oh, and we thought we were
the bees knees. Jenny went on the fella's motorbike. And we were
standing in the corner and I thought we were going to get a hammering for her. So we come in and my mother says 'Where's Jenny?'
and Da had a boat that had just come in and he's lying on his bed.
He says, 'Where's Jenny, she no in yet?' I says, 'A fella gave her a lift
on his motorbike. He was going to give her a run.' And Aggie men-
tioned the chap's father's name. And my father jumped out of his
bed and she said, 'Get out of here the now till he got his trousers on
and his shirt', and he says, 'Right, I'm out', and he went out after
him and Jenny cam' along the road waving to him, and 'Stop that
bike' he says. Well he run and got Jenny, flung Jenny off the bike,
and pushed the fella away again and my father – that's the only
time I can mind of my father, took her by the shoulders and shook
her. Her heid was going backwards and forwards. He says, 'You
never go on another man's bike for as long as you live.' It was some
chap that had worked on the boat and he had said, there wisnae a
lassie that he hadnae had anything to do with. My father never
wanted his daughter to get blackened in that way. So Jenny never
went on a motorbike again. My mother says to her the next day,
'Look at your coat, hen, it's all oil up the back with his exhaust of
his bike.'

*Her mother's strictness, as Helen understood, fought with a desire
that her daughters should have some fun in a way that was denied to her.
Financial pressures and the early arrival of children after marriage meant
that for many young women courtship was the freest and most enjoyable
time in their lives.* My mother was strict. My mother used to let us go
dancing and sit and wait for us coming in to get the news, how did
we get on. Who did we get lifts from. She lost her young life from
getting married to him so the result was she used to more or less
listen to our conversations. She hadnae had much of a life herself
and she had to bring us all up so therefore she never went dancing.
She kept us back but in a sense she didn't.

4

Getting Married and Setting Up Home

We had a quiet wedding. Well my dad was working and
my husband was out next morning.

*In the first half of the twentieth century the expectation for most young
women was that they would be married, and their upbringing and education had prepared them for this role. Engagements generally lasted some
time. The woman was usually working during this period but there was
a strong convention that she should stop when she actually married.*

*Because of the large numbers of young men killed in the First World
War the opportunity of marriage passed some women by, while a few
others made the choice not to marry – though unmarried women were
often stigmatised as 'old maids'. A natural progression to the state of
marriage could be interrupted by other responsibilities, as it was for Mrs
Gardiner:* If my mother felt ill – she died with kidney trouble, and
she must have known she wasn't going to get better, because she
always asked for me, 'If anything happens to me will you look after
the family? So I said, ' Yes'. So I made my pledge to look after the
family and I saw them all married before I got married. *Mrs Gardiner
eventually married when she was thirty in 1912.*

GETTING ENGAGED

*Engagement was an important stage in the process of settling down, and
could last some time while a couple saved up enough to rent and furnish
a home of their own. Molly M. from Glasgow was unusual in by-passing
this:* I got married when I was eighteen. I was out with him three
times and run away to get married. Well, he stayed with an uncle
who died so I was able to walk into a house in Mill Street. ... Well I
daresay if I hadn't ran away and got married I would be like the old
song 'Getting Married in the Co-operative Hall'. My man ... was a
different religion from me. I just went out with him three times and
decided to run away and get married. I just wanted to be out the
way that was all, so I got married at the Registrar's Office.

Liz Kent recalls the night in Glasgow in 1931 when she became engaged. We met when we were seventeen at a dance hall in the Clarendon. We used to get away tae the dancing up there, an' he wis saying 'This is ma girlfriend' – he wis that proud o' himself, ye know. One o' the men said 'Well away an' take her down for a walk to the marriage place.' ... It was a sort of path and there were things over it an' there were flowers there and they called it 'the wedding walk.' An' he says 'Well that's what I'm gonna do, I'm gonna walk right down there and that will be our wedding walk.' Ah says 'An' when dae ye think it's gonna be oor wedding?' *They married at Hogmanay.*

Mrs Bruce's recollection of her engagement in the 1920s touches on some important issues: asking father's permission to marry, saving up for the wedding – and a man's tendency to put football before everything else! I must have been about eighteen then and of course we hadnae any of ma things saved up. That's when I went into Melrose's, I just used tae put the tea in the boxes. I was engaged by this time, but it was a while before I was married. I wasnae married till I was twenty-three. I was engaged, and my engagement ring was bought in Leith Provident Store, I had had my eye on this ring for a while.

There was a row that day that we bought it. He was a great Hearts man – he was Hearts mad till the day he died, and he wanted to go to the football match the day we were getting engaged. I hadn't got permission from my dad to put ma Sunday suit on – well you had your Sunday suit and your weekday suit. An' ma dad was very strict and he asked, 'What's Sunday suit on for the day?' I says, 'Well we're going to get engaged today.' 'Nobody asked my permission.' 'Well he's going to ask you tonight.' That was the story. When we got to the store he said to me, 'Will ye go and have a look at that ring an' see if it fits you.' Well, I got my engagement ring and got it on ma finger and he says, 'Oh that looks nice, you'll no get anything nicer than that.' I says, 'I'll just take it', and I was all dressed thinkin' I was going out for ma tea. He says, 'Wid you mind very much if I jumped on a tramcar and went to the match.' Of course, I nearly exploded and I didnae want to go home 'cos I knew I wid sit and cry and ma dad wid be angry. So I had to walk about all Saturday afternoon till it came to teatime and then come home. An' of course I still had the ring in ma bag. When he came down for me at night to go to the pictures I threw the ring at him. I said, 'Now that's your ring', I said, 'If that's how you're wantin' to carry on, that's it, that's it finished, I'm not having any more to do. I don't want your ring.' However, eventually he got me coaxed round to go to the pictures and in the pictures of course he gradually got round ma soft side, got the ring put back on ma finger in the Gaiety. So that was ma engagement. An' then of course we got married, oh it's about four year later I got everything collected, got married about four year later. In 1928 I was married.

It was the convention that a girl would leave work when she was married and her workmates usually clubbed together to mark this rite of passage, as Greta Connor recalls: If you worked in a factory, a few months before, you'd get a book going and collect so much for a present and so much for taking the bride out.

However, in many cases the fun did not stop there. Bette Stivens, born in 1917, has uncomfortable memories of some of these rituals: When you got married there was this form of entertainment. They used to dress you up in fancy hats, embarrassing things, dirty jokes here

18. A girl tied to a postbox in Glasgow as part of the celebrations before her marriage, c.1950.

and there. I'm afraid I slipped out and disappeared very quick, the day before they thought I was going. Actually they caught me and I locked myself in the toilet and never came out until they'd gone home. In factories they used to make you wear a chamber pot and crepe frills around your neck and you carried that through the town dressed as a bride. That to me was very embarrassing.

THE WEDDING

It was usually only the better-off families that could afford to provide their daughter with a dress that was only going to be worn once. After the Second World War white weddings became more common, but before that although some married in white most girls wore a dress that became best and Sunday wear afterwards. Elizabeth Freel was married in Duke Street Church, Leith in 1930: I was no white bride, I had a nice pink dress. *Mrs Bruce remembers:* I just had an ordinary dress. A black velvet that I wore and a white collar on it, that was all I had. We didnae have very much money in these days.

Ina Laidlaw married Bob Hutton in July 1931. She can recall the exact cost of her wedding dress. I wore a long bridal gown and Bob looked handsome in his stripes. The material for my wedding dress was figured crepe which cost two and six [2s 6d] per yard. It required 6 yards, 15 shillings, plus the dressmaker's charge of 6 shillings. The total cost was £1 1s 0d. The veil cost £1 1s 0d and the satin shoes were a real bargain:12 shillings reduced to 6 shillings.

During the wars, there was little time for planning, and weddings were often hastily arranged, as for Mrs Jamieson, who married during the Second World War. Well he was in the army. You see the war started and we got engaged. The war started in September and we got engaged in October, and he was in the army, he was in the army right from when it started because he was in the Territorials. I got married in January 1941, down in Coburg Street, in the Harper Memorial. I had absolutely nothing, because my husband was stationed at Lee-on-Solent, and he was being sent abroad, so he got embarcation leave ... I got this letter on Hogmanay, and that's when you had two or three posts in the day. He says, 'I'm getting my leave starting on the 10th of January, can you make it, arrange it to get married?' That was it, snow and ice. Well we were in mourning you see, after my brother had been missing for six months. That's what

19. The white wedding of Bob Hutton and Alexandrina (Ina) Laidlaw, July 1931. She remembers precise details of the price of her dress.

I was wearing, black you see ... Well, I was really torn, I really was. I didn't know what to do, afterwards I said to my husband, 'Do you think we should have waited?' And he said 'No' because he had no desire to have a big wedding or anything like that.

In the first quarter of the century a simple wedding ceremony was often performed in a house rather that the church. Frances Milligan describes the practice in the tightly-knit community of Newhaven, in north Edinburgh. It was a community wedding with the near and dear and they didnae have tae go to the church. They werenae usually married in the church, but in the manse maybe, in front o' the company, in the house or in the Fishermen's Hall. *As Stanley Jamieson suggests, this practice of marrying at home died out after the Second World War.* A generation earlier than us were married at home. Not by the Forties, we weren't married until 1948, but in the 1920s and 1930s a lot of people were married at home. The minister went up to the house and married folk. *A common alternative was for the couple to go to the minister's house, the manse, as Mrs Cowe of Leith recalls:* I mean it was just like getting married in the church, it was the Minister that married us, but we got married in the manse. See long ago people got married in the manse. I don't think there were any registrar houses, like what we have now in Ferry Road.

20. A newly married couple outside a Partick church, after the Second World War. Getting married in best clothes was still common at this date.

Leither Mrs Bruce, married in 1928, remembers her wedding at the manse vividly: We was married on a Friday, and it was a weekday and of course Saturdays an' weekdays wis all the same because my husband had to work on Saturday in the morning. They worked till one o'clock on a Saturday in these days. It was a Friday night, at seven o'clock, because the men were working till five or six o'clock. Then we had to go to the manse – get a taxi then go to the manse and come back again and we had a wee bit celebration in the house, that was a' for oor wedding.

The minister was sitting with his feet on the mantelpiece: I'll never forget it. He was sitting with his feet on the mantelpiece, well back on the settee with his feet up. An' the maid knocked on the door and turnt it and let us in, 'Yer party, Sir', an' the minister just turnt round and looked – well he near died when he saw us. I heard him give her a telling off in the hall, 'You ought to have warned me, you ought to have known I might fall asleep'. An' when he came back he said, 'I'm very sorry about that,' he says, 'I'd fallen asleep, I make no excuses, I'd fallen asleep.' Then of course he sat and lectured us aboot the sanctity of marriage and what not: did we know we what were moving into an' how long had we known each other? Of course he knew all that because we used to be church members. We'd left a taxi standin' outside an' the man hooted. He said, 'Don't tell me you've got a cab outside there'. ... An' my brother said, 'Yes.' He says, 'Oh! that'll do now'. He got the bible right away an' the marriage was done quickly an' we got shooched out the door for the sake of getting in the car. My brother had said to him, 'Just wait', thinking we wouldn't be five minutes in the manse and we must've been quarter an hour to twenty minutes in the manse, an' of course the taxi meter was running up all the time.

Some people were married in a church, and these weddings became more popular after the war. Peter Rennie was married in 1949. It was December the 9th. And it was also the first night we had snow for a' the winter. And I remember the wife wi' her big train goin' doon the church, it was covered wi' slush and snow. After the wedding we went to Coltart's, the photographers in Leith Walk. That was more or less the nearest photographers. Pretty good one for weddings. And as the group stood posing for the camera a' the lights fused. We were left in the dark!

After the Second World War Registry Offices were becoming used if there were religious issues or a couple wanted a quiet affair. Edinburgh and Glasgow both have keenly felt religious divides and marriages between Catholics and Protestants could cause serious family difficulties, as for Molly M. My man was nine years older than me but that wasn't the issue because he was a different religion from me. ... I got married in the Registry Office. ... Because I had been a Catholic and missed going to mass he agreed to get married again and let me get married in the chapel but we got married in the vestry and he had to promise that any of the children of the marriage would be brought up Catholic ... But getting married in the Registry Office it was. We went in a taxi to the Registry Office and then we went into a place called Granny Black's in the Candleriggs. We went in there and had a breakfast ... I was married and I said to him, 'Is that it?' He said, 'Yes that's you married.' I just thought this was terrible. I wasn't married as far as I was concerned.

Another Glasgow woman remembers: Me, my husband, my sister, her man and two friends went out to Bailiston Registry Office. We had a brilliant day and stayed out too late. We had everyone up in his mother's house waiting for us.

CELEBRATIONS

As weddings were often small affairs, having them at home avoided the cost of hiring a hall for the reception afterwards. The parents of the bride usually laid on the meal, sometimes with outside caterers. Elizabeth Freel, married in 1930, remembers: My mother, she was going to have the wedding in the house, but she was called to my brother's. His wife had had a wee son unexpectedly; it came before its time you know. And that was that, we got everything ready, we set our tables ourselves. Scott Lyon, they catered for us and my mother baked a bit. We had an urn of tea. We didn't have much drink. *David Anderson remembers his wife cooking for house weddings in the area:* There were a lot of house weddings in these days. My wife was a cook, she made most of the trifles, and a couple of bottles of whisky would do in those days.

Nettie S. from Bridgeton, Glasgow, had her wedding at home in 1950: My other brother got married in the February a couple of months after me so she had two weddings in October and February. My wedding was held in the house and they made steak pies, totties and peas. It was two accordionists and a drummer in the room with a big table in the middle. They had to clear the table away

21. A wedding breakfast in a Partick home, Glasgow, c.1950.

after everybody ate their steak pie and totties. My mother's sister's daughter's man played the accordions and that was our band. It wasn't like this day and age when you had your honeymoon and flew over to Spain and that.

If the wedding party was large a couple could be married in a tearoom or hall where they could also have the reception. This was for economy as well as convenience, as Norrie Campbell of Edinburgh explains: My father and mother were married in a tearoom up at the North British Hotel. Churches were expensive, paying for the decoration, the beadle and organist. *Ina and Bob Hutton were married at Old St Paul's Church, Edinburgh, in 1931.* We had 42 guests but no music, as the church organist also played at the Capital cinema, and we couldn't afford his fee. The reception was held in the Fife Rooms, Great King Street, which was considered quite posh. The menu was steak pie or salad, followed by jelly and ice cream or strawberries and cream. All for the princely sum of four shillings and sixpence per head. The whole reception cost about £10 and this included a four-piece band.

Stanley Jamieson's parents came from Leith, but he and his wife had their wedding reception up in Edinburgh. We had our reception in the Balmoral Rooms in Princes Street. Very toffee-nosed! Well, it was a reception, it wasn't just a meal and that was it finished. Yes, there was always a reception afterwards with dancing and games and singing, and all that kind of thing.

The Temperance Movement was still strong between the wars and many weddings were dry. However ample drink did not appear to help the tension at Mary Holligan's wedding: I had been engaged to Dennis for about one year. My mother booked the hall, and engaged the band, a five-piece band. We had a nice big cake, plenty of beer, whisky and wine, all this in the Thirties too. The wedding reception seemed to be fraught all the time, as there was this feeling of tension between the in-laws. I was, I'm afraid, more concerned about all this than my new husband or the guests. *After the Second World War, it was more usual to have drink at the reception. Peter Rennie remembers:* The reception was held in my wife's house. One memory o' that is we had a firkin o' beer – what ye called a firkin o' beer was a barrel. And I remember my Auntie go astride o' it as if it was a horse!

Although many of the old marriage customs of rural areas were not followed in the town, some vestiges can be seen in the fishing community

71

at Newhaven. Mary Johnston describes the Scots tradition of handsel: a gift brought good luck to a new beginning. I mind someone in our family and the wedding celebrations went on for two or three days after it. Often you used tae show your presents off in what was tae be your new home. So you were showing your presents and your house off at the same time, that's when the house was handseled. You handseled the house with a gift. *Sandy Noble also describes celebrations going on for several days in Newhaven.* Very often friends would come up to the house early and bring their presents up. There was celebration and talk and that was another gathering and tomorrow the other cousins would come from the other side and they brought their gifts and it made it a week or a fortnight of celebrations. *Gifts would usually be of a practical nature: bed linen or crockery. Christina Turnbull remembers her best gift:* Oh when I'm getting married I got a new, oak wooden tub. It was one of the nicest wedding gifts you could get.

The wedding reception was also an opportunity for the local children to collect a few pennies, as Isa Keith remembers: I think it was probably when they were leaving the reception, and they'd always have a handful o' coppers and they would throw it oot the taxi at the kids. The kids would all gather round and shout 'Poor oot', that's what they'd shout 'Poor oot.' They came fae all over, they always knew when there was a wedding. *Charlie Bescow remembers* If they didn't pay, all the kids used tae shout 'Hard up!' Oh aye, that was another way of getting money, find out where the weddings were.

HONEYMOON

Before paid holidays were introduced few men could take time off work and it was not unusual for them to go back to work the day after they married. This was the case for Mrs Bruce, married in 1928: We had a quiet wedding. Well my dad was working and my husband was out next morning. He worked from six until twelve of a Saturday. That was their hours. And my father worked night shift. That must have been one of his night shifts. *Dodo Keenan recalls that Friday evening was a popular time to be married:* If you went to a wedding on a Saturday afternoon it was very posh – it was usually a Friday night.

If the man was in paid work and the couple were able to plan their wedding, the Trades holidays in July were a popular time to be married,

22. A 'scramble' for coins at a wedding in Partick, late 1940s.

as David Anderson explains: And they'd try to leave it till Trades Week when people were on holiday so they didn't lose pay, for their honeymoon. *Many couples couldn't afford to go away, especially between the wars, and would maybe make do with a celebratory meal and a night out. Margaret Christie's mother did not even have as much as a meal when she married in Glasgow in the 1940s.* My mum went out for margarine and came back married. Yes that's what she done.

The practice of going away on honeymoon became more commonplace after the Second World War, as Stanley Jamieson says: It was usually a Friday and then you went off on your honeymoon on a Saturday. It was just because Friday night, people could get off work maybe and come to a wedding and it was obviously a convenient time to start, you know, a week or a fortnight in a hotel thereafter. Well this was by the Forties again, yes, post war years. Between the wars a lot of them quite certainly didn't go away for their honeymoon.

Ina and Bob Hutton did go away on honeymoon in 1931, but accompanied by Ina's mother. My going away outfit was a blue dress and bolero and the latest 'Amy Johnson' blue coat. We left the reception about 6pm catching the Aberdeen train with my mother. We were to spend our honeymoon with her. We did manage an outing to Banchoray, made the best of things and enjoyed ourselves.

Often the need to keep earning meant that if couples did go away, it wasn't very far. Peter Rennie married in 1949: As far as honeymoon went, just a case o' going to my brother-in-law's prefab at Northfield for the weekend, so's I could get back to work as soon as possible.

STARTING MARRIED LIFE

People married because they were in love or thought they were in love, and to assume an adult life independent of their parents. Girls brought up to be morally correct rarely experienced intimate love or expressed their affection physically before they were married. Respectable men were expected to wait until marriage and would not force themselves physically on a woman. Mary Holligan recalls how she felt at her wedding. I can say I got the best when he chose me. But being young at the time I didn't seem to appreciate him. I loved him, he knew that, but the funny thing was we could never express it verbally. I could never show my affection for him: I wanted to but I was afraid my mother would not like it. So all through our courting days, and after the wedding in the village hall it all seemed as though it was all like going to a party ... I couldn't think I was a bride, and leaving the home

Many young women were unprepared for their wedding night. As emerged in the first chapter, the facts of life were hardly ever discussed at home and girls were often kept in a state of ignorance, like Mary Blackie, who was married between the wars: When I got married I didn't know anything about men. He courted me for four years and I didn't even know what my great-grandchildren can now say is a man's penis. I didn't know anything at all about it. *Elizabeth Dawn was the same:* I was very ignorant as well. I was married when I was twenty and it was after that, that I found out I was ignorant. I didn't know what was in front of me.

It was not only in the area of sex that young women were unprepared. They may have helped their mother around the house, but that didn't mean they were able to run a budget and a new home. Molly M. describes the experiences of her wedding day in Glasgow: I remember [him] giving me a lot of money – he worked for himself, he had his own business, six pounds ten [£6 10s 0d] for a wage, that was a lot of money. I hadn't a clue what to do. So when I came off the car, they went to the match, me and my best maid went into Cochrane's at the corner and I spent all the money on food, and I hadn't a fridge at that time, just a cupboard – tinned stuff, you name it. I just thought that was the done thing. So when he saw it he said 'What are you going to do for the rest of the week?' Oh I never thought. So I shouted a boy from across the back on the Monday and they took the suit that I got married in to the pawn ... That was my first and last, I knew what to do with money after that.

If a couple had managed to save up they might have been able to move straight into a place of their own. Many however had to move in with parents, relatives, or a neighbour who had space for lodgers. Peter Rennie married in 1949: We went to stay with my mother, who had then moved to Greenside [Leith], for about seven years. That's how long we had to wait for a Corporation house in these days, seven years. Eventually we got one in Colinton Mains. *Nettie S. didn't have a house to go to when she married in the 1950s in Glasgow.* When I first got married we had nothing, we didn't even have a house. It was just one of these kind of weddings. You were brought up kind of Victorianish, your mother never told you anything. She was too busy wondering how she was going to feed us the next day. I was married out of the house. After the wedding we didn't even know where we were going to stay. I was going to stay at an old uncle's, he was the last in the house, he didn't get married until he was fifty-four.

In the Sikh community a newly married couple was expected to live in the family home. For Kulwinder Kusbia this was a good experience: I lived with my mother-in-law: I had five brothers-in-law, two sisters-in-law, my husband's grandfather and his grandmother and we lived in Tennant Street, in Edinburgh. It was two room and a kitchen and we all lived there together very happily. There was no running hot water or anything, we used to heat the water up on the fire. On Saturdays the tin bath would come out to bath all the kids ... And they'd all get sat on the bed and we'd make tea, it was really nice, I really enjoyed that. We all stayed there for nearly two years and then we moved to a bigger house. And by that time I had a son and a daughter. We all moved together, the whole family moved to a bigger house.

The first house for a couple, usually a one-room single end, was special, as Nora Cruickshank from Glasgow explains: I was sharing a house with the in-laws before we got the single end. It was always a place of your own, even if it was just a single end. It was smashing because when you were sharing with in-laws it is not so hot, but to get your own wee single-end, it was great. *For Jan Well however a single end was claustrophobic.* I came from the South Side to the Gorbals and after I got married I went to a single end in Lawmuir Street. I came out of a room-and-kitchen and in a single end I just felt totally closed in. I couldn't stay in it. *Although single ends were recommended only for newly-weds and single people, many couples continued living in them with children, as Cathy Dodwell remembers:* It wasn't till after I was married that I was in a single end. There was five of us, our three children and ourselves.

For some the new house was a first taste of personal space. Many couples didn't have much furniture to start with. Margaret Thomson from Glasgow remembers starting out like this in the 1940s. It was great. After sharing with a brother and two sisters at home it was great. You didn't have any furniture, what you did have was a kist that your mother kept all her blankets and sheets in and that was our table. *Elizabeth Freel rented the furniture for her single end in Leith:* There was only room for a small amount of basic furniture. We had a room above the Rubber Mill in Leith Walk. It was two an' six [2s 6d] a week, two an' six a week for a' our furniture out of Brown's across the road. We had a sideboard, table and chairs and a bit linoleum, a wee carpet at the fireplace and a wee fender thing.

Ella Williamson felt quite well off. It was just one room with a little kitchenette and a toilet. It was really not too bad for first off in these days. We had our own toilet. Well, there's houses in Edinburgh yet that some have to share toilets so we were really quite lucky. ... We didnae need an awful lot, just having the one room. We had a bed-settee so it looked like a sitting room when anybody was in. It was big enough to take a bed-settee and two chairs and our dining table, which closed up, gate-legged, and the four chairs. We had what we called a bed closet, you know you could put a bed in it, but we had wardrobes in it where we hung our clothes. It would be '46 because we went and stayed with an aunt for a few months and then we got a house, a prefabricated house, which was lovely.

5

Having Babies

You had your family after you were married because you
did not know how not to have a family.

*Once married, respectable women would not undertake paid work outside
the home. Instead their role was to keep the home and care for the children who would be expected to arrive before too long in the days before
effective contraceptives. Home births were common during this period.
Having children was seen as a woman's business, though for some it
might have seemed like a woman's burden. May Carson puts it bluntly:*
They just had babies. They just lay and had babies. I mean my
mother and father. There were six o' us to begin with but two died
and there were only four of us eventually ... As I said to ma mother,
'What on earth did you get out of life?' But you see there was
nothing very much in life.

BIRTH CONTROL

*Before the advent of the contraceptive pill in the 1960s women had few
choices in limiting their fertility. Dr Mack of the Family Planning Clinic
which started in a shop in Govan, Glasgow in 1926, sums up contraception as:* a choice of unpleasant methods and you have got to choose
the one that is most suitable for you. There was no ideal then, there
is no ideal now.

   *While there were women's clinics in both cities from fairly early in the
twentieth century and birth control advice was available, for instance at
the Women's Hospice set up by Elsie Inglis in 1902, few women were
able or willing to access such help. Jane Patterson, a Medical Social
Worker in Edinburgh, born in 1919, saw women worn out by repeated
pregnancies.* They had very little rest from childbearing. Contraceptives were rather frowned upon, although the family planning clinics were getting going ... You got female pills from the chemist, and
you took these and you would have a miscarriage.

Helen Dunbar, born in 1940, who worked as a young midwife in both Glasgow and Edinburgh, recalls one woman laying down the law after too many births in the family: I remember one granny, it just so happened that her four daughters had all had babies in the last year and of course the granny has been running around witless after them. The last one in particular had had a very difficult birth – we thought she had lost the baby, and it was very tiring all round. I just happened to be in the house the day she summoned her four son-in-laws to say she had had enough. She said, 'We're having no more babies in this family. For the next two years there's to be none, it's just lust and we're not having it.'

Although Catholicism expressly forbade the use of artificial contraception some older women who were Protestants also felt it was immoral and unnatural, as May Carson vividly suggests of the 1930s: You were bad if you used contraceptives at that time. You really were, by Jove. Freddy says to me, Freddy says – we're only six weeks married when I fell wi' Jean – he says, 'Oh if it is as easy as this, I'm going to do something about it ...' And he did! And we have ten years between her and Freddy. But ye were supposed to be bad. I mean yer Granny wouldnae ... oh she would have been horrified. You would be a street walker to her. You would just be a streetwalker if ye were doing anything like that. It is not human. It is not right.

Helen Dunbar remembers methods used in the late 1950s and 60s: Coitus interruptus was the commonest form of contraception – as they said in Edinburgh 'Getting off at Haymarket'. There were condoms but that was for the man. Pessaries were quite common, Lendle's pessaries, if they remembered to put them in in time. The

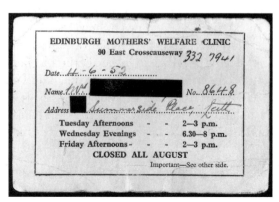

23. The Edinburgh Mothers' Welfare Clinic gave contraceptive advice along with other services: a card from 1952.

pill was just coming in but some women were a bit scared of that. They did practise control of a fashion ... The working-class woman was quite prudish about the area between waist and knee. ... It was referred to as 'doon there'. There was this kind of Calvinistic thing of non-interference with nature as far as contraception went.

Some women refused to use artificial contraception on religious or moral grounds even when repeated pregnancies put them at risk. Dr Libby Wilson visited women in the tenements of Glasgow during the 1950s: There were some people whose only method their conscience would allow them to use was the rhythm method so we had these 'year at a glance' calendars and I used to mark the days of their periods and then I would put green for go circles round the relevant days up until the mark of the red cross which was the no go days and then green for go after that. We used to visit them every month until they got the hang of it. ... There weren't many who used the rhythm method but we tended to see them because they were the women with large numbers of children.

In order to encourage women to use contraceptives, health workers from the Domiciliary Family Planning Services set up in Glasgow in the 1950s visited people in their own homes. Home visits saved women having to travel to clinics and allowed an informal relationship to develop. Dr Wilson again: We used to put these coils in, in people's houses, and they worked terribly well and we never had any problems, they were so relaxed in their own house ... There was this big fat lady. I don't remember how many children she had but it was about five or six. So she just managed to lie across the bed because those beds in the wall are not terribly wide, she had her legs up on the edge of the bed and her head against the wall. She was smoking a fag and had one of the kids lying across her tummy. I was kneeling across the floor ... the floor was absolutely filthy. The sister I worked with had a bit of purple carpet from her bathroom floor and she used to carry it around in her bag so that I could kneel on the floor. So I was kneeling on this carpet and was poised ready to go in, in fact I was just about to insert, when this huge Alsatian's head came out from underneath the bed. I was terrified. The woman just said, 'It's all right love, he'll no' hurt ye!' I thought here I am assaulting his mistress, he could easily become aggressive. I was really frightened!

PREGNANCY

Girls ignorant of the facts of life had little idea of what pregnancy entailed. As Mima Belford, born in 1918, puts it: You had your family after you were married because you did not know how not to have a family. *This Glasgow woman was not unusual:* When my first child was born I didn't know what happened. I thought your belly button just opened up. I was quite innocent, right enough. *Even as late as the 1960s, Christine Quarrell, who lived in the Queen Elizabeth flats in the Gorbals, did not understand what was happening to her, aged sixteen, when she was pregnant with her first child.* I did have my mother and older sisters but it was taboo and nobody talked about it. I was constantly confused about which hole the baby was going to come from. As far as I was concerned I had two openings in my body and they were both for waste material and nothing else. I was sure I would die and I was sort of prepared for that. I was completely immobilized with fear.

Joan Williamson knew the tell-tale signs: If you missed your period once you were worried, if you missed it twice you were sick! I was sick mornin', noon and night, for most of my pregnancy. They said it must have a lot of hair to be upsetting ma tummy, and she did, lots of black hair. When I fell pregnant I went up to Simpson's and the nurse said, 'How long have you been married?' I said 'Ten weeks'. I must have fell pregnant as soon as I was married. I was like an elephant.

Mothercraft classes like those remembered by Greta Connor from the 1930s were more concerned with looking after baby than preparing women for the birth room. We had ante-natal classes in Leith. You had your mothercraft classes about what diseases you would expect a baby to have. It was in South Fort Street. I used to go every Tuesday and we had classes and we had examinations and you got a prize.

As the birth process became more medicalised after the Second World War there was more encouragement to attend ante-natal classes. Joan Williamson went to the clinic up at Simpson's [the maternity wing of the Royal Infirmary in Edinburgh]. They had relaxation classes up to a certain number of weeks before the birth.

Women's health was depleted by years of childbirth and poor diet, and it was hard to establish patterns of pre-natal care, as Alice Hick, a dis-

24. An antenatal relaxation class at Torphichen Street Clinic, Edinburgh, 1963.

trict midwife in Edinburgh, recalls as late as the 1960s: You got an awful lot of cases with no warning, or perhaps they'd just seen a doctor a couple of times, something like that and many of the mothers were in very poor condition. You know, quite anaemic: the clinics were building up but there were still an awful lot of women who never bothered to attend.

Some women had dramatic stories of when their waters broke. Marion Mackintosh was queuing: I was in a long queue, queuing for oranges when ah went into labour. I would not leave until I got my oranges. I had queued so long for them. *Stella Curry wanted her money's worth at the pictures:* I was in the pictures when I went into labour. I had paid tae see the movie so ah wisnae leaving till I had seen it.

GIVING BIRTH

After the introduction of the National Health Service in 1948 an increasing number of births took place in hospital. Before this children were more likely to be born at home, probably in the bed they were conceived in, and home birth was still a common option in the 1950s, as Helen Dunbar recalls: It was the accepted thing to have the baby at home. These lassies had been around when their mothers and sisters had been pregnant and had had babies and though they hadn't done it themselves they knew about it. They'd been involved with it. It was still very much a woman's thing with the midwife and the mother and the granny, the support was there.

The birth was essentially a domestic affair attended by female relatives or neighbours. There was always a local woman skilled in the birthing process who might be called upon. Betty Hepburn's mother was one such: My mum helped to deliver babies. Maybe if the nurses were late she would be asked to go and help. There were lots of women who could help each other out in their confinement. There was always a woman on the stair doing all the washing for a few shillings. *Men were largely absent, and certainly did not see the delivery, as Alice Hick says:* The men would be out of the house – we rarely saw the husbands. Sometimes they were there, they could be very helpful, but they wouldn't be there at the actual delivery – not at all. The students were there but we had to call them Doctor all the time 'cos doctors were accepted but any other male was not accepted at all.

Helen Dunbar is eloquent on the value to tenement women in the past of an extended network of women supporting them. Birthing was a woman's thing, children were a woman's thing. I think in some way women have lost out on the company of women in women's things. It used to be shared because everyone about you was in the same boat. Women used to meet round the close mouth and have a wee natter. Now they have to seek women's company. The mother wasn't isolated. Her sisters, aunties, mother were all around to help.

She attended many home births. There would be Corporation cars laid on to take us out to a case, because you had to take the gas and air machine with you and the little black bag that had the babies in it according to the children! When you got to a single end you always carried a candle, matches, a shilling for the meter and four pennies for the phone. Everybody knew the nurse had a shilling in her pocket, when the lights went out: 'Have you a shilling for the meter Nurse?' Unless the baby was about to be born you held on to your shilling, they always had one by the meter anyway. The other children would be in the other room, or if it was a single end, farmed out to the neighbours who took them.

Norma M., a health visitor in Glasgow in the 1950s, remembers: On the midwifery level many of the beds were hairy, and I mean hairy in every sense of the word as they were hair mattresses and there were pets as well. Often the woman would be in a lovely dip in the bed and what I would do is take a dining room chair and literally take the seat out and put the women's bottom on that so at least we would have a smooth rigid surface.

Midwives also had to consider religious differences and sectarianism in Glasgow. Helen Dunbar here remembers in detail attending a family in the Gorbals: I had gone late at night to deliver the baby and as one does, the minute you go into the house you glance round the walls to see if it is the Sacred Heart and the Blessed Virgin, or King Billy and the Rangers Team. This was a Catholic household so I thought, 'Fine, it's Parkhead and not Ibrox.' You had to watch how your conversation went sometimes. ... It was a big box bed and you usually had to climb in to get deliver the baby. She was a bonnie, bonnie lassie in her early twenties with golden red hair hanging loosely around her shoulders in curly ringlets. All during labour she prayed between contractions for a healthy child. Now I have heard women calling to God in their labour – they'd frequently say, 'Oh Jesus God, when is it going to be over?' But she actually prayed that she'd have the strength to bring forward a healthy living child. Once the baby was born, before I'd even cut the cord, I held it up between her legs and said, 'Look, it's a wee lassie', and the first thing she did was to reach out and bless the baby and blessed herself and thanked God for a healthy living child and I felt so privileged. It was beautiful. Then once I'd cut the cord and washed the baby, Dad came through with the two boys and they climbed on the bed beside Mum, and Dad came in with three glasses and said, 'Will ye wet the wean's heid nurse?'

Home births could allow the women a greater mobility during labour than the more regimented hospital births. Sometimes we actually had them out of bed and on their hunkers. There was one old doctor in the Gorbals and if things were not going right he'd say, 'Right nurse, go back to the Bible, get her on her hunkers.' So we'd spread newspaper out on the floor and she'd squat down the way nature meant you to have your baby and frequently the baby popped out no bother at all. It's not easy to lie on your back and push.

The doctor or midwife would attend at some point during the birth and, before the advent of the NHS, a charge was made for each visit. Greta Connor from Leith remembers with gratitude one doctor who did not collect the fee. I had my first child at home and your confinement was four guineas. I had this lady doctor and I asked her, 'What about the bill?' and she said, 'Don't bother about bills. If I take it off you, the taxman takes it off me.' I had both bairns free. That was Margaret Munro. She was well known for it.

Helen Dunbar describes the role of the midwife under the NHS, and remembers 'her miracle'. Usually in home births the doctor would pop in at some point. If there were any difficulties you contacted him. Sometimes you phoned the doctor and he would be away seeing to someone else and you just got on with it. Often by the time the doctor got there whatever was going to happen had happened. I went to listen to the heartbeat and didn't hear it one time I listened. ... He [the doctor] couldn't hear anything either, but said he'll just see how things went ... Well it was about two in the morning when the lass rolled over and said, 'I think I want to push.' She gave birth to this baby which was sort of a navy blue, black colour. What you did at that time was to cover it. You didn't give them the dead baby like you do now. And it sort of twitched. I don't know why, maybe it was involuntary so I sucked it out and this was my miracle. She lived. I slapped and slapped and got all of the muck out of her and she began to breathe and her colour changed from a sort of navy blue to white and then pink and she survived. We didn't expect her to. The doctor was quite surprised.

However such miracles were rare, and infant mortality within the tenements of the inner cities was high. It was commonplace to lose at least one baby or have a child die in infancy. Emily Batten from Leith had twin daughters of whom one died when she was nine weeks old. It was a great shock to me and it took me a while to get over it. Many, many months.

Poor living conditions had a marked effect on the survival of mother and child. Many women died in childbirth of complications such as puerperal or childbed fever. Jane Patterson explains: They had been malnourished all their lives. They'd had very little rest from childbearing but I think they were exhausted by poor physique to begin with, too many children at too rapid intervals and maybe even having to go out to work, going out as a cleaner or something like that.

After the Second World War hospital births gradually took over from home births, although there had been lying-in provision in hospitals in both cities for at least a century beforehand. The Rottenrow, for example,

25. Mothers and babies with nurses on the balcony of Elsie Inglis Hospital, Edinburgh, c.1925.

Glasgow's main maternity hospital until the 1990s, was originally founded in 1834 as the Glasgow Royal Maternity Hospital. In Edinburgh the Simpson, planned as a maternity hospital in 1879, made way in 1939 for the Simpson Maternity Pavilion, part of the Royal Infirmary. The Elsie Inglis in Abbeyhill, a popular and respected maternity hospital, opened in 1923, was closed in 1988. The cost put many women off using the hospitals. They had to find the tram and bus fares to get there and before the NHS had to pay for the confinement. Barbara Anderson paid some 'three pounds odd' for her daughter Helen's birth at the Elsie Inglis in the mid 1920s.

NEW MOTHERS

As Helen Dunbar emphasises, having and caring for babies was a woman's thing. Even with the growing insistence on hospital births women would be expected to care for each other's babies, as Stella Curry remembers: I remember I was in hospital in labour and the nurse handed me somebody else's baby to feed. And I said, 'I don't feed anybody else's baby', and she just laughed and handed me the bottle.

Nan P. recalls this distressing attitude when she was in hospital during the Second World War in Glasgow. When there was an air raid in Rottenrow the nurses would give ye your baby to shelter in your arms. So you couldnae go to the shelter. You had to stay in bed. My baby cried the whole time and I couldn't feed him because I needed a nipple guard and the nurses wouldn't come round until after the air raid. It would go on for an hour, maybe longer. They gave me someone else's baby once and I was shouting that it wasn't mine and I could hear someone shouting the same at the end of the ward. They were saying it doesn't matter but they swapped them over and we got our own babies to shelter.

She remembers the regime which kept babies apart from their mothers most of the time. You only saw your baby at feeding times. The baby was always taken to the nursery after feeding. *Breast-feeding was generally encouraged, as Bette Stivens, who had her baby during the Second World War, attests:* You only got to use a bottle in hospital under medical supervision. It was the done thing to breast-feed. You almost had to get written permission to bottle-feed.

Breast-feeding was said to make for healthier babies, and was also seen as a form of natural contraception, according to Madge Earl: Some people breast-fed for a year. You see they had the idea that they wouldn't get pregnant. *Fashions changed and breast-feeding waned in popularity during the 1950s as part of the process of modernisation and an emphasis on science and hygiene, aided by the marketing practices of the multi-national formula milk companies such as Nestlé. Bette Stivens remembers:* When you had your baby there were firms that looked up the birth columns and then you got all this paraphernalia sent to you.

Women who were not breast-feeding had to have their milk stopped, an uncomfortable process as recalled by Nan P.: Brown paper and vinegar poultices were used to stop your milk: you bound up your breasts. This was in the days before they came up with the pills to scatter your milk. *There was prejudice against breast-feeding among respectable women on the grounds that it was 'dirty' and their husbands did not want other men to stare at their wives when feeding. However formula milk needed to be hygienically prepared under conditions rarely possible in the old tenements. It was also expensive, so that some babies were undernourished as mothers economised to make it last.*

New mothers, whether their babies were born at home or in hospital, were expected to spend about ten days in bed. Alice Hick, working in Edinburgh, remembers that rules were difficult to enforce if the women were at home: We were dealing with the really very badly off people and they didn't want to leave home because they had no one to look after their kids. We'd get into fault trouble with Sister Mackenzie because she used to insist that the mothers had clean sheets on every day and of course we used to visit for the first few days I think it was. Twice a day for the first three, and then visited once a day if it was possible to the tenth day. Mothers were supposed to stay in bed during that time. That was the same in hospital. See in hospital you kept them in bed for nine days and let them up for the tenth. It was wicked of course: by that time they had lost their legs, you know, and they really felt desperately tired. But of course on district mothers never stayed in bed ... They used to know roughly what time you were likely to arrive, they'd be lying in bed, but every now and again you knocked on the door and there'd be a scuffle, and she's out of bed again. And you'd go in and there's the whole kitchen steaming with washing. When we asked them if they had clean sheets, they were always, 'Oh they're at the washing', or 'My neighbour took them to the wash.'

Professionals had to be pragmatic about what people could afford. Norma M. of Glasgow remembers: There was no point telling a woman to get something if you knew in your heart of hearts that she did not have the money. There was quite a bit of demonstration like bathing baby and how to care for the umbilical chord, which terrifies a lot of mothers.

Women would normally have the support of family and neighbours who made sure a new mother was coping, as Helen Dunbar describes: She wasn't left alone with the baby. When the baby arrived some-

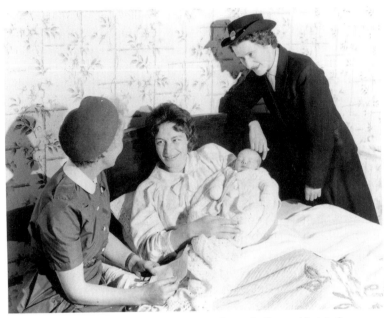

26. After a home birth in the early 1960s the midwife would visit the mother for fourteen days, after which she would hand over to the Health Visitor.

body would come out and say, 'I've made some soup and I'll take your bairns away' or they'd take the washing away and it would come back ironed. It was an extended family, there was less post-natal depression then. Mother's weren't so isolated. You couldn't go two steps before some old wife stopped you to give advice and say, 'What a bonnie wee baby you've got'. Or there'd be an old granny who'd heard him and would say the next day, 'Oh I heard him last night. That sounds like colic.'

However Alice Hick highlights a couple of occasions where women were clearly very much alone. Other mothers could be censorious, particularly of women who were thought to neglect their children. In most cases the neighbours would be quite helpful. Though of course they weren't always there. One of the nurses that I know told of going out to a case at night, and there was only the mother and one small boy in the house, and she had sort of to shove the boy out of the way while she got on with the delivery. And then she went back a day or two later, the small boy was being bad and the mother said to him, 'If you don't behave yourself I'm going to give the baby back to the nurse. She can take it away the way she brought it, in her wee bag.' 'She didn't bring it in no black bag, my mother peed it!' He'd been peeping through the door all the time.

And there was another one that never got help. I think probably that the neighbours had got fed up, as she was completely useless sort of thing. She just couldn't cope with anything. I think if I remember rightly her husband left her. There was one little boy and he'd either be wearing a jersey very torn and battered or be wearing a pair of pantaloons. I never saw him with both on at the same time. No shoes of course. And there was absolutely nothing in that house, we even had to go and knock up a neighbour to get some tea to make a cup of tea after she'd had the baby, and she'd just nothing. She should never of course have been able to have it at home ... there weren't as strict rules.

Some women certainly found it very difficult to cope with the new experience of motherhood, as Mary Holligan admits: I often wonder how I managed through the first years of married life. I often think my husband never realised how I felt, the trauma of post-natal depression. I didn't want to go out. I just seemed to let myself go. Yet I tried to behave normally.

It was a matter of pride to maintain appearances despite emotional struggles. Busy mothers had little time to indulge their feelings and besides, many of their friends and neighbours in the tenement communities would be going through the same life experiences. Dr Lunan of the Rottenrow suggests why there was little complaining: Women were just so happy to have survived childbirth, and if they had gotten a live baby out of it even better. It was not uncommon for women to lose their first baby or even have their own lives at risk with a first pregnancy.

ADOPTION

Some couples were left childless despite their strong desire to have a family. On the other hand many unwanted babies were born. Norma M., talking of the 1950s in Glasgow, remembers: It was easier to adopt babies in those days. There was plenty of them. You understand that there was plenty of them because contraception wasn't as good or as reliable and the services were unavailable in many instances to unmarried mothers ... Some clinics wouldn't see single girls. It was pre-abortion so these factors meant there were more children born to unmarried mothers. Some were kept in the family, if you like, and often granny would take on the responsibility and rear the child as if it were her own and the girl would go back to work. Some went out for adoption of course.

Women suffering the pain of childlessness might take an active role in bringing up other people's children, or might seek to adopt a child. In the early twentieth century babies were frequently advertised in the local papers for fostering or adoption. In the Miscellaneous column of the Edinburgh Evening News for 29 April 1910, for instance, alongside adverts for the removal of superfluous hair, were the following:

> CHRISTIAN couple, no children, in country, would adopt baby, no after claim; state premium.
> PARTY wanted to nurse healthy boy, 1 month old, £1 monthly.
> RESPECTABLE party with superior home would take walking child to nurse; 18s monthly.
> RESPECTABLE party, adopt baby from birth, middle of April; no premium. No after claim.
> WANTED, male child to adopt, healthy, of good parentage; small premium; good home guaranteed.
> WANTED, party to adopt healthy baby girl, 2 months old, no premium; no after claim.

In 1911 Mary Holligan's mother tried to adopt a baby advertised in the Evening News. Mum kept working at the mill, and as the years went on there were no sign of any babies, which disappointed my parents, but one day a woman in our village adopted a baby – which was a great surprise in those days, as no one knew at that time how one got those babies. So she asked the lady, who was a Mrs Kay, how she had gone about it, and she said one had to watch the *Evening News* for there was a column called Miscellaneous, which advertised children for adoption ... So my parents kept looking for the column in the paper. Then came the information they were looking for – a child for adoption in Edinburgh, off Nicholson Street. They went up to the city and met the mother of the baby who wasn't born then and the woman promised to give them the baby when it was born. However as the time went on there were no letters or messages from Mrs M. My parents had purchased a cradle, pram, baby clothes etc. in preparation for the baby. On the day they decided to go up to Edinburgh for the child the aunts and neighbours did on a nice party to welcome the child. When my parents arrived at the house, when the lady opened the door they could see the baby clothes hanging in the house. They knew the baby had arrived and the lady told them they couldn't part with it as she had promised before seeing the baby, a little girl. My parents were very upset and seeing my mother crying so bitterly she offered to give my mother the little girl for one year. But my mother refused as after seeing the child through teething etcetera she would be more attached to it then would have to give it back to the lady. My mum could hardly get downstairs stumbling through her tears, but a miracle happened to my mother though she didn't know it at the time. I was born four months later ... it was a great occasion when I was born. The Christening parties went on all week

Not all children were adopted by childless couples. Mary Holligan's mother went on to adopt two small children. Mum was 47 when they arrived. Ruth I think was two and James three. I accepted them as my own although the youngest brother to this day is filled with resentment at me, never visits me. But I was the one who had to work hard to help to bring them up. It was one menial job after the other and hard jobs, some of them.

Some children put up for adoption came from married women economically or physically incapable of bringing up another child. Mary Holligan's mother also fostered children who were waiting to be placed in new homes in Edinburgh. There was very little supervision over adopting children. ... Mother was instrumental in getting good homes for a lot of children round Portobello and The Jewel and Newcraighall. I was never told by my mother that she was going to get children. Father never seemed to interfere, and I would come home from school and there would be children in the house. I was never told their names or where they came from.

Religious agencies such as the Guild of Aid and the Salvation Army offered support to all women regardless of denomination. Although the Glasgow Guild of Aid was Christian it was not sectarian, and both Catholic and Protestant women used their services, although Jewish women did not. Benefactors gave from all over Glasgow to support their work and the Guild placed babies all over the country, as Marald Grant recounts:

27. A young Glasgow woman and her baby, c.1930.

At that time when I came there weren't any adoption societies at all. I had an awfully nice person who lived at the Art Galleries [Kelvingrove, Glasgow] and she kept the babies for me if they were illegitimate babies and she got them homes. I once went to a place near London to take one down. They said we weren't to speak outside ... because no one was to know that it was a child from Scotland that they were taking. There were a lot of babies adopted. ... I took the babies when they were very young.

The years of the Second World War allowed women greater freedom to travel and mix freely with men. A heightened sense of living for the moment meant that there were inevitably babies born to unmarried girls during this time. Parents keen to avoid social shame were desperate that the mother's identity would be kept secret. Somebody came to see me, and her husband had been head of one of the big firms in Glasgow, a very well known person. And they had three daughters and it was wartime, and the youngest daughter had joined up and she was down in the South of England, and when the raids were on and that sort of thing, she was in an underground shelter, and she and this young man were left alone in it on night duty. And the result was that she came home and was to have a baby. They were in a terrible state about it. At that time it was a simply appalling thing to happen. So they came to see me to see if they could have the baby adopted, and have it attended to so no one would know. So they had sent the girl up to Caithness or somewhere and she was in a hotel until it was time and then she came down to Edinburgh. At that time, my assistant Miss Williamson had a friend who had been married quite a long time and had no children and was desperate to get a baby. We thought this would be an awfully nice home.

They said I had to promise that no one would ever know a thing about this. It had to be done absolutely quietly. So I quite agreed. The thing was that we were to take the baby away whenever it was born. The girl wasn't to see the child. The baby was born at night. We got a phone message and I was away at about 11 o'clock. The girl was awfully upset when I went in. The sister had been told how the baby was to be taken away and the girl was in such a state wanting to see her baby, that she took her in to let her see the baby. She was terribly upset and I was ill myself. She was really desperate. However, we just had to come to take the baby away. I got a very nice home for it. The girl gave up her work as a nurse and everything.

Once the baby was with the new parents the birth mother had to live with her loss and mourn in secret. All contact with the child was severed. Marald Grant placed over forty babies during her time with the Guild. Inevitably some babies were the consequence of extra-marital affairs. I knew who this girl was. She lived quite near my brother in Crookston. The girl got married and she had a baby and her mother came in to see if I could help. The difficulty was the husband didn't know anything about anything. She must have been pregnant before she got married and he was away at the war. I was to get rid of the baby, to take it away, so that he would never know that she had had the baby. And then I got a phone message to go at once, and she was in an awful state, and she said that her husband was getting home a week sooner than we had arranged to take the baby away, and she didn't know what to do. ... She asked me to break the news to the husband which was a very difficult thing to do. But he didn't give tuppence! He said, 'I'm not even interested'. I nearly dropped. He said 'As long as she is fit to get up and go with me and have a good time, that's all I'm caring about.' I was to take the baby away and that was all that was in it. She never said goodbye to her baby.

One traumatic case for Mrs Grant was finding a home for a baby born of sibling incest. I didn't know what to do. I was nearly demented. A doctor sent this person to me ... she said she had a son and a daughter. They lived in Ibrox, and she and her husband used to go out on a Saturday night, and the boy was two years older than his sister, and she always left him in charge. And through time the girl was having a baby and she was only fourteen. And her brother was the father I didn't really know what to do. We waited and the time came when the baby was born. It was a lovely baby.

I had a man come down ... and they were down for a baby. I had no other. This was the only baby I had. He would come down and ask, 'Is there not a baby yet? Have you not got us a baby?' And I wondered. I didn't know if it was legal or not. You couldn't put it away. You couldn't destroy it. It was beautiful baby. What I did was, I said, 'Well Mr So and So, if you wakened up and found a baby on your doorstep, would you take it in?' 'Oh', he said, 'I would be delighted.' I said, 'I found this baby, and I can't tell you who was the mother, or anything about it, but I've got the baby.' I said, 'This wee child was found without any information.' He said, 'You know from whenever you told me you'd try and get me a baby, I started a bank book, and I've got a nice bank book ready for her.' The child went into the most wonderful home. It haunted me for ages. And I thought, 'Dear knows where that child would have been put, had I reported that.'

Respectable working-class girls who 'fell' pregnant might have strong moral or religious objections to abortion even if they were aware enough to seek one in time. However up until the Abortion Act of 1967 many back-street abortions were carried out, often resulting in infertility or even death for the mother. In later years effective contraception and legal abortions meant that that fewer unwanted babies were born. The decline in the authority of the church and the easing of state attitudes towards unmarried mothers also meant that some women felt able to keep their babies despite the lingering social stigma of illegitimacy.

6

Feeding the Family

Mum would wait to see everyone had some first ...
She looked after the family first and was last to get
what there was.

One of the main challenges for a mother was how to feed a large family adequately on a low budget. Meals were plain and simple, and food was usually fresh, as there was little way to keep it. Women demonstrated a great ability to stretch a few ingredients into a substantial meal. However it was not unusual for the mother to stint her own portion in order to feed the children.

The shortage of food during lean times is remembered keenly, but meals are also spoken about with great nostalgia and often pride: granny's scones and mother's sheep's heid soup were family legends, and recipes were handed down from mother to daughter. Certain food was associated with particular occasions and played an important part in the celebration of high days and holidays.

FAMILY DIET

A housekeeping budget of 1913 (appendix, p.186) gives a breakdown of the food purchased during a typical week. Beef and vegetables feature every day and would have been served up in soups and stews. The staples are porridge, bread and jam, and potatoes. The only additional protein is one pound of haddock and a pair of kippers or a quarter pound of cheese for a family of two adults and three children.

The day started with breakfast – porridge, milk and bread were an essential part of the diet. Margaret Thomson, growing up in Glasgow after the Second World War, remembers : We always had porridge for our breakfast. Sometimes before pay-day we would come home lunchtime and it was maybe porridge for our lunch. I am not saying we were dead poor, but we weren't rich by any manner of means, but at least you always had a meal. On pay-night we always went to the chippie for a fish supper or whatever.

95

28. A young woman learning to bake oatcakes on a girdle over an open fire, at one of the classes run by Edinburgh Corporation to train young women in 'useful' skills, 1928.

Bread was bought every day. It was often the children's job to go down to the baker's, as Norrie Campbell, born in 1912, remembers: We never ate bread, which was only one day old. When sent to the baker I always asked for 'old bread', that is, had been baked the previous day, and it was always plain bread. *Mary MacKay has a similar memory of the Southside of Edinburgh:* We lived in Nicholson Street and we were sent to a baker's in the Pleasance with a pillow-slip so we could get the second day bread. *Bread was essential for filling up. The practice of throwing a 'piece' out of the window to the child in the street or the back green or back court below was common in both cities, and is remembered with nostalgia by families who moved into high-rise flats. Joan Croal recalls:* Porridge in the morning, with bread and jam if you were still hungry. Bread with your soup at lunchtime. And then when you came in from school, a piece and jam. And the same when you were out playing – you shouted up for a piece and they'd throw it out of the stair window to you.

Soups and stews were an economical family staple. Bones from the butcher were boiled to make a stock to which could be added any combination of barley, lentils, rice, oats, or dried peas, supplemented with potatoes, carrots, leeks, onions and turnip. Soups could be full and nutritious if vegetables were available, or thin and watery.

As Phemie Anderson says, the family's diet was very dependent on income: I don't think we ate such large quantities as today, because when we were wee things were hard, money wasn't there. You just had to buy a bone and make your soup, and it had to do you two or three days maybe sometimes if your father wasn't working.

The pot of soup simmering on the fire became a symbol of neighbourliness. Frances Milligan prided herself on her sheep's heid soup: Every Sunday morning at 6 o'clock I'd get five people that can't make it themselves, and give them all a jam jar of soup. *A large cast-iron soup pot was a permanent fixture on the side of the range in Margaret Hepburn's memory:* There was always a pot at the side of the fire, either the stock pot which contained either a knuckle bone, or a sheep's heid, and it was either broth or potato soup we had. Maybe there would be a stew pot containing rabbit, or a piece of mutton, which was normally cooked with butter beans. *A few families worked an allotment which could produce a steady supply of vegetables for the soup, as in Phemie Anderson's case.* I remember my mother made great soups. She was famous for her soup. My father had an allotment where we got vegetables from.

Meat, mainly beef, was made to go a long way. Olivia Wilson's mother was skilled at this kind of cooking: My mother could make a pot of soup out of practically nothing. You could get a piece of brisket, make a good broth to feed a family two, maybe three, dinners out of the piece of brisket. She made quite a lot of stew and she would buy a piece of sirloin. ... Chicken was expensive, you see. Beef wasn't so expensive and women bought the beef and minced it for shepherd's pies and mince and tatties.

Dodo Keenan's mother was well known for making potted meat: In the summer time she used to get meat, a bit o' hough an' a bone, and made potted meat, an' you had potted meat all week. She used tae make a big load, an' she was that well known for her potted meat the neighbours would say 'When you're making potted meat, Mrs Campbell, would you keep me a bowl?'

Another speciality was potted sheep's head, described here by Isa Keith: They would give you a sheep's heid, they would cut it in half and it had tae get a lot of cleaning before you actually cooked it. She'd clean and clean it, and then she'd leave it overnight in salt water to make sure it was absolutely clean. She used tae take the tongue and cheek, she would press it in a plate, ken, a dish, and then a plate on top and maybe the iron, and press it. And that was potted head. It came out like a pot, ken, wi' a jelly. It was potted head, but no like the stuff they sell now – it was real potted head and it was lovely. And you'd have that with beetroot for supper. She'd use the head for making soup, sheep's heid broth, that's the nicest soup you could ever have.

Isa also remembers the labour intensive work of cleaning the sheep's stomach when her mother made tripe: Ma mother used tae buy a sheep's bag and we had tae clean it as children. It was only a six-pence. It took a lot o' cleaning. Ma mother used tae boil cauldrons of water and we used tae have tae scrape and scrape wi' knives, scraping this tripe, you know and wash it and wash it and scrape and scrape. And then she would boil it over and over again tae make sure and then she would cook it, and it was lovely.

Fresh fish was in plentiful supply in both cities. Dodo Keenan remem-

29. A woman sitting next to her range in the kitchen of a Glasgow tenement, c.1920s. The fire provided constant heat for cooking. Behind we can see the curtains of the recessed bed.

bers having fish regularly at teatime: Fish, we always had a bit of fish, herring or haddock or cod. We never got fish as a main meal, because we always had our dinner in the middle of the day and if we had fish, we got it for our tea: likes o' kippers, or potted herring. Ma mother had a friend that worked down in Leith in the place where they dried the cod, and she used to every so often get three salted cod for one and six [1s 6d]. Ma dad used tae cut them up, they were tough, and put them in a pail cut up intae pieces, and let them steep until they were soft. Then she boiled them, an' boiled potatoes, and she wis famous for her fishcakes as well. He loved her fishcakes, so we often got these, but I never liked fishcakes.

Betty Hepburn describes how stovies, another basic meal, were made: To make stovies we'd use roast beef dripping, loads of onions, but don't let them get brown, then slice up your potatoes and keep mixing them all through, keep mixing them and then add just a tiny drop water and put the lid on and cook it very slowly. Once it's softened, put the sausage or corned beef in and let it cook on the hob.

Clootie dumpling was a traditional dish, but usually reserved for special occasions. *It is a pudding named after the cloth or cloot in which it was cooked. Mary Holligan describes her mother's:* She always made clootie dumpling – flour, currants, sultanas, treacle, sugar, suet, orange peel and sixpences. She also added spices. She floured the cloth and put in the puddings. It was put on a plate in a large pot to boil for one and a half to two hours. It used to be lovely and moist.

ROUTINES AND TREATS

The routine of the weekly meals for some families hardly ever varied. Dodo Keenan's mother had fourteen children and out of necessity had a pattern of family meals that hardly changed each week. Dodo remembers it in wonderful detail. We had bad times, but we never starved. My mother was quite a plain cook. I knew from one week's end to another what I was going tae get for ma meal every day.

Well, on a Saturday we had pies for quickness at dinnertime so as my Dad could get to the football match. Teatime was usually fish, bananas or cheese. Ma Dad used tae like red pudding, or pig's trotters. And then on a Sunday morning we always got a sausage, bacon and egg. Ma mother always dealt with Campbell's

30. The British Argentine Meat Company started as a wholesale agent in 1914. Soon after the First World War the company ran retail butchers all over Edinburgh and Leith. Beef was the cheapest meat at this period.

the butchers. You got sausages for five pence a pound and ma mother had dealt with him since before the First World War. And the van man used to deliver the butcher meat: there were no fridges in these days. Saturday – and he used tae bring the sausages and either stew or tripe and a piece o' meat. And we always had the stew on a Sunday; and we didn't get that until about three o'clock, and sometimes we got trifle. We always had our evenin' meal, our supper at about eight o'clock because we had tae go tae the church, half past six tae half past seven. And then when we came home from the church, it was boiled ham or a bit roast pork on a sandwich. And she used tae get, seven for thruppence, chocolate open biscuits at the Store.

On the Monday you got the rest o' the stew, but she always got a bone or somethin' tae make soup or a sheep's head and it was always broth on a Monday and a Tuesday. At teatime we got what was left o' the sausage an' bacon. On the Sunday she would pot-roast this piece o' meat. Well, on the Tuesday, after your soup, you got a bit o' the cold meat. If you were lucky you maybe got a veg with it. And on the Wednesday she always made potato soup with the beef jelly from the pot-roasted meat, and you got the rest o' the cold meat.

On the Thursday, that was washin' day, that wis the Lord's My Shepherd's day, because you didnae have that much. And you'd have the second day's soup again, and if there was some of the cold meat left she made a shepherd's pie; and if not, it was just stovies, just made wi' some o' the roast beef drippin', the potatoes and onion, no meat or anything. We always got a cake that day. An' then, she always washed the butchers' aprons, the manager and his son, and she always used tae take them up on a Thursday, and he would pay her for doin' that, maybe two shillin's, half a crown. But he always gave her, even during the wartime he done it as well, two or three chops or somethin' like that. So it all depended, what you got frae the butcher, we got for our tea that night.

And on a Friday she put in her order, you see, for the Saturday. In the middle of the day she just used tae go to the butcher along the road. An' it was usually mince, an' occasionally liver an' a veg. And we always got a puddin' on a Friday – it could be rice, it could be custard, a wee tin o' the cheapest fruit you could get, semolina, or she'd make pancakes, you know, pancakes wi' syrup. We got these curds, curds an' whey, we used tae have it wi' sugar.

The weekly pattern of meals was repetitive, but efforts were made to make Sunday a day with special meals. It was treated as a day of rest on which to go to church or visit family, and the expectation was of some treats. The day usually began with a fry-up, as Elsie Tierney recalls: On Sunday you always slept late. Then when you got up about eleven you'd have fried sausage, fried bacon, a bit of black pudding and sometimes a chop. Then later on in the day, about seven o'clock you'd have boiled ham and tomatoes and maybe a cream bun!

Mary MacKay remembers her mother cooking a large Sunday lunch:
On Sunday we'd have dinner about two o'clock. My mum would
make soup and cook a piece of rolled lamb, potatoes and vegetables. And then a bread pudding, with the old bread of course. Every
Sunday we had a three-course meal. *Mary Holligan was a miner's
daughter and remembers Sunday meals with relish:* On a Sunday when
we came home from church, Mother had a large saucepan simmering of sausages, onions, thin sliced potatoes and lots of gravy. It
was all very tasty, with big floury potatoes. We also got bread and
jam pudding, all plain meals, but wholesome and filling.

*Christmas was not given as a holiday in Scotland until after the Second World War. The tradition of eating roast turkey for Christmas dinner dates from the 1950s, but the food for Christmas Day was usually
special – perhaps a chicken, as Olivia Wilson comments:* Of course you
didn't get chicken except at Christmas, chicken was expensive you
see. *New Year was a much bigger holiday with the food to suit the
occasion. An Edinburgh woman remembers:* To eat, black bun and
shortbread marked off in sections. and a tongue. Steak pie for New
Year's dinner or a piece of silverside. *This was an occasion on which
some people who didn't have ovens would take their food to the baker's to
be cooked, as another Edinburgh woman recalls.* My mother used to
buy the meat and put it in the pie dish with the gravy and we'd take
it along to Mason's the baker. and he would make the pie crust, put
it in the oven and you'd collect it later ready. It was beautiful flaky
pastry. You used to get a jug of gravy too, the gravy was lovely.
They used to stay open till late, late, late on Hogmanay.

Margaret Hepburn remembers the special treat of a clootie dumpling.
At the New Year we really had a blow out – either steak pie with a
jug of gravy, tongue, or potted hough and there was always a clootie
dumpling. On all our birthdays there was a clootie with small silver
charms in it. A button, that was a bachelor; a doll, that meant a
baby; a ring, that meant a wedding; a bell, that meant a wedding; a
thimble, an old maid; and a silver threepenny, that was riches.

BUYING AND STORING FOOD

*There was very little storage facility for food in the house and it was
bought on a daily basis from local shops. Women had their regular sup-*

pliers: the butcher, grocer, greengrocer, and the Co-op or 'Store'. Many women would shop nowhere other than the Store. Most produce could be bought at the grocery and some Stores had a separate butcher or fish-monger. For more on the importance of the Co-op see p.147.

In Edinburgh the fishwives from Newhaven and Fisherrow in Mussel-burgh used to come and sell fish around the streets, and this became a part of many families' weekly routine, as Betty Hepburn recalls: We used to have the fishwife come from Musselburgh and we'd have cod's lugs for fishcakes on Friday.

Town dairies were situated in many areas of the city and fresh milk was delivered from hand-pushed or horse-pulled carts. Small milk cans or jugs were taken out to the cart and the milk was poured in from the churn. Mary Gilchrist remembers this: Milk, I can remember when I was in service, there was a girl came round, she had a barrow of milk. You told her how much you wanted, and she poured it. I

31. The Cumnock Creamery Company at Morrison Street, Edin-burgh, c.1924. It was run by Dodo Keenan's sister and her husband. The milk was delivered around the streets from the handcart.

think the Co-op was the first to deliver it, in glass bottles with a wide mouth. But every street had its own wee dairy.

Elsie Tierney from Newhaven grew up near a town dairy. We lived opposite Mr Watson's dairy and saw the milk being delivered. The farmer brought the milk straight from the farm on his horse and cart every morning. He delivered a five-gallon churn very early in the morning. The farmer would leave it on the pavement outside the dairy, then carry on delivering his milk to the other dairies in the district. When I was sent for a pennyworth of milk, I would take the jug and go to the dairy, push the door and try and get in the shop and shut the door behind me before the bell above the door stopped clanging. I would give Mr Watson the jug, he would take the top off the churn, put in a half pint measure, fill it and pour a pennyworth of milk in the jug.

Food was usually cooked as soon as it was bought. In summer it was difficult to keep it fresh, as Joan Croal recalls: There was very few refrigerators at that time, so you had to buy food fairly often, usually every day. Some people had a piece of marble, you called it a cold slab, and milk and butter would stay on that you know, for a day or two. Either that or fill a bowl of water for your milk.

Refrigerators made a huge difference when they became generally used – though some women, like Margaret McDonald's mother, as she recalled in 1993, never liked the idea of them. She only recently got a fridge, I remember we used to stand our milk bottles in the big, deep sink with the water. It was really embarrassing because all our friends were these modern people with fridges and washing machines and electric irons. We offered to buy her things when we started working but she just didn't like electricity. She felt dubious about electricity. If it was thunder and lightning, everything got unplugged.

In winter the room was usually so cold that food could be stored in there. Betty Hepburn describes other arrangements: I've seen people use a box with wire netting over it for meat or anything and you put it out on the edge of the window. Then you just opened the window and went into it. ... You kept everything in the press covered up, because of mice, you put lids on everything.

Women were so used to buying fresh food that they were sometimes, like Betty's mother, suspicious of tinned food. We always had fresh

32. Mrs Jeanie Thomas, in her kitchen in Gourlay Street, Springburn, c.1945.

food. My mother thought tins were poisonous. I always wanted to taste tinned beans. And when I was about ten I got invited to a birthday party and we had beans on toast, and oh really! I thought it was great.

Olivia Wilson's mother was similarly doubtful about frozen meat when it arrived in the shops. Then there was a butcher's shop opened, it must have been about 1925, and this was frozen beef from Argentina. And my mother was frightened to try, and then a friend said, 'Well, I'm going to buy a piece of sirloin, see how it is.' And after that my mother always bought a piece of meat from the frozen beef shop, because it was about half price.

MEALTIMES

In most families breakfast was eaten between 7am and 8am. The midday meal was 'dinner', between 12 noon and 1pm when the school age children came home. They might have had a piece – bread and jam – when they came in from school in the afternoon, and 'tea' was some time after 5pm. In many families the children did not eat at the same time as the adults: it was common practice for the father to be fed first, as he was the wage earner. Christina Turnbull remembers this, though her family always sat down together. The men worked very hard and I know lots of children, you would see their father going home and you would

say, 'That's your father away up', and they'd have to wait till he'd
had his tea – the father would have his tea before the children. But
my father, we all had to sit down together when he was at home.
The family all had to have the same. *Helen Nickerson's parents only
allowed the children to eat at the same table once they were earning a
wage.* We never sat doon to the same table as my mither and faither,
never. If you worked you got to sit at the same table. My mither and
faither sat at the table their two selves and then each one as they
grew up got to sit at the table.

*The father usually had the largest portion or extra protein, as Mrs
Fairbairn's did, on the grounds that he was the wage earner.* Well, we
used to get sent to the butcher's with a penny to get a marrowbone.
And when she made lentil soup she got a bit of mutton and your
father got that for the meal, wi' a potato,'cause he was out working, but you only got the plate of soup with bread. He was the
breadwinner, and he got a wee bit extra because he was hard worked.

*While father had the largest portion, mother usually had the smallest,
even though she also worked physically very hard. Joan Croal explains
the way it was:* At mealtimes, you watched to see what you got, but
father got the most. Father got served first, he was the boss, he was
the working man, he brought the money in. He had a chair all of
his own, your dad, you weren't allowed to sit in his chair. Mum
would wait to see everyone had some first. She often had less than
what you had and made up with vegetables. She looked after the
family first and was last to get what there was.

*Manners were usually drummed into children at mealtimes. Children
were expected to be seen and not heard and misbehaviour was usually
not tolerated. Mary MacKay recalls:* I used to get sent out of the room
for giggling. I sat in the wardrobe in my bedroom and giggled myself out. *Children were frequently punished for poor table manners and
the ultimate sanction was going without food, as Betty Hepburn attests:*
Elbows on the table! 'All joints on the table will be carved.' 'No
eating peas with the knife!' You had to hold your knife and fork
properly if you were at the table, and if you didn't it was the bigger
knife your dad had in thae days and you'd get a nick over the knuck-
les. And if you didn't do what you were told you'd get sent from the
table – 'No food'.

7

Yer Ne'er Done

**It came down from your parents you had to keep cleaning,
they were always cleaning, your Granny especially.**

*Life for tenement women was a constant round of cooking, cleaning and
washing. Electricity did not really begin to change work in the home
until after the Second World War, when more conveniences began to be
used. Before this even simple tasks took longer. Water was boiled on the
coal fire; washing was done by hand in a tub. High standards of cleanliness
were a mark of respectability and women struggled against all odds
to maintain them. There was constant pressure to keep up appearances.
In a tenement infection could travel rapidly and there was a real fear of
spreading germs. Consequently anything that could be was scrubbed and
polished. The repeated view is that 'you didn't have much, but what you
had was spotless and shining', and people had a real sense of pride in
their homes.*

*An overwhelming memory of many people is that their mothers
never stopped working. Isa Keith, born in Edinburgh in 1919, remembers
the laboriousness of the old ways of doing things.* I think oor
mothers had a tremendous amount to do. You know, they don't
know they're living today and good luck, but ma mother, I don't
know how she accomplished what she did. She made oor clothes,
she knitted oor jumpers, she had a huge washing. She used tae be
up at the crack o' dawn, she was never in bed before twelve at
night, before midnight. No washing machines in they days to do
it. Everything had to be done the hard way; you had tae boil up
your water and you had the old-fashioned stoves tae clean and no
facilities like they have nowadays. It was hard work, very hard
work.

*Most families lived in houses of one or two rooms and an enormous
amount of time and effort was spent packing away the beds in the morning
to make room to move. Mary Laird of the Women's Labour League
gave this pertinent evidence to the Royal Commission on Housing in*

1913: The labour expended in keeping a one-room house in order is out of all proportion to its size. It is a constant succession of lifting, folding and hanging up, and if this is relaxed for even a short time the confusion is overwhelming.

CLEANING

If a house had a water supply it was a cold tap in the kitchen sink – most Glasgow tenements had this facility. But some women, particularly those who lived in the older converted properties in Edinburgh, had to go out for their water. Elizabeth Freel, born in 1908, had to carry water up to her attic in Leith. We got a wee attic flat in Duke Street. Four [storeys] high, outside toilet, outside water – you scooped it out of a pail wi' a ladle. *Stella Stewart from Edinburgh remembers:* When I was a child in Brown Street we had no water in the house. We had to go to a tap that was in the hallway outside the stair. There was a sort of sink. I don't know what colour it was, because it was pitch dark and you could never see it because there was no natural light and no gas light. We used basins to carry that water. My mother heated water on a fire on a range.

Pat Rogan gives a salutary reminder of the burden on women in the poor living conditions of dilapidated tenements that he visited as a Councillor for the Holyrood area as late as the 1950s. This brings me back to my point about maintaining cleanliness and this idea that 'We may have been poor, but we were very comfortable and cosy' – it's just not true. Their life was hell, it was a constant daily grind against dirt and disease. While it is true that people worked very, very hard to keep themselves and their property clean, it was nevertheless a constant struggle.

Weekly tasks were often done on a Friday so that the house was clean for the weekend. Jenny Petrie remembers how she wasn't allowed out until certain jobs were done. Friday night was Brasso night. You didn't get out to the dancing till the brasses were done, candlesticks, even the taps. We used to get the shelves cleaned and new paper put on a Friday night. Blackleading was done on Friday night too. Once a week you got a packet of blacklead. You broke it up and mixed it with water. Then you put it on with a brush, let it dry and then you polished it. A velvet square was used for burnishing it.

33 & 34. Images of tenement women doing housework are rare: the pictures taken by Alf Daniels of his wife Irene toiling in her spotless Partick kitchen in the 1940s are a valuable exception, even if they sometimes look rather posed.

Polishing was often a child's job, as Joan Williamson recalls: My dad got this burnisher made. It was leather-backed with steel hoops all sewn together onto the leather. You used to burnish the knobs that go along the front of the range. When you finished up, they looked like chromium. Then when you got on a bit better you actually got them chromed – even your ash pan – and that cut out your work a bit.

Richard Goodall remembers a joint family effort: We had all our work to do. We had to keep the fireside, all the tongs and shovels that were all, had to be polished and the hearth had to be pipe-clayed. The shelves of the house where all the dishes as we called them, china, they were taken down and thoroughly washed and put back again for to be clean on the Sunday. That was once a week. It was most remarkable for a family to be so tightly bound in a house of that nature.

Cathy N., who grew up in Glasgow after the Second World War, took it for granted that she as a girl had to do a lot of housework, but it affected the way she brought up her own children. Six in the morning, we used to have to get up before we went to school to do our chores. It was typical, though, the boys didn't do anything. Mum worked so we had to do the cooking, cleaning, everything. You couldn't go out until you had everything done. We were used to it so it didn't bother me. I made up my mind, maybe it was right or wrong but I didn't let my kids do anything. I did everything for my kids right up. I didn't want them to have to do what I did.

High standards of cleanliness were handed down as in Betty Hepburn's family, and entailed endless work: It came down from your parents you had to keep cleaning. They were always cleaning, your Granny especially. Everything had to be in its place and a place for everything. When I went to my Granny's I had to clean the flues. You had to keep the house spotless. Scrupulously clean!

After Barbara Anderson had her baby she tried desperately to keep up with her usual cleaning routine: I was cleaning the range and the sweat was running down and the nurse said 'Now that's ridiculous. Put those things away and get dressed and get out and take the baby with you. It will do the two of you good.' She says, 'There'll be plenty o' rainy days to clean the range', which was very true.

The linoleum on the floors was scrubbed and the rag rugs were taken outside to the back green and beaten, as Betty Hepburn recalls: You just had wee rag rugs and linoleum. You had to wait till the washing was in and you took them down to the green. We were given the beater and told to get out and beat it. You didn't need a carpet beater to beat the rugs, anything would do. I've seen them use a tennis racket or a cricket bat and knock nine bells oot o' them. There wasnae any vacuum cleaner, because you didnae have carpets. They progressed from a rag rug to a small rug.

Many women didn't get a vacuum cleaner until well after the Second World War, along with a carpet, as Joan Williamson explains. Most people didnae have a carpet until the Fifties and Sixties when you were able to afford a four by three [yard] carpet to fit your room, with a surround to polish up. If you got a four by three carpet, you decided you were going to get a vacuum cleaner as well. You wernae goin' to go on your knees for a four by three carpet! *Betty Hepburn thinks that some tenement dwellers were ahead of the well-off in turning to labour-saving appliances.* All the posh folk were a lot later in getting their hoovers. In fact until their servants were cut down they didn't bother getting labour saving gadgets, they had servant power.

An important step towards labour-saving was the installation of electricity in the tenements. In the early part of the century houses were lit with gas, as Betty Hepburn recalls: The gas mantle was so fragile. Every time you wanted to do something your mother would say 'Light the mantle' and as sure as guns the taper would go straight through the mantle and you would get slayed and it was usually when the shops were shut. In 1948 we had electricity put in, you had to pay for it yourself, it was £10 for a room-and-kitchen. You had to ask permission from the landlord and he had to vet whoever it was you got to do it. My mum's next door neighbour was an electrician and we got it done on the cheap. There was four on the landing and he said he would do it if he did the four. It was only one junction box so that cut down the price for them, so the four on the landing were done at the same time. They got sockets and a central light, one in the room and one in the kitchen, but none in the toilet. It was terrific, you could do so much more in the evening – sewing, mending, knitting much easier.

The vacuum cleaner was hailed as a labour-saving miracle, but did it actually free up time? Bet Small thinks not. Labour-saving devices don't save you labour, because if you have a vacuum cleaner you do other jobs as well. I think we did just as much work as our mothers did.

One reason for almost obsessive cleaning was a constant fear of infestation by the 'wee beasties'. This was almost inevitable given the close proximity of dwellings and the age of the properties. Bed bugs would infest the beds at night when the occupants were there and during the day they would move back into the walls and picture frames. Pat Rogan remarks: Until the arrival of DDT the bulk of these houses were infested with bugs, fleas, scabies and lice. Nothing much could be done unless you could move the people out. But when the big clearances started down to Pilton and Granton, Prestonfield, Craigmillar, Craigentinny, it was a prerequisite then that when they moved your belongings they were placed in an enclosed van, taken away and disinfected. *The new Corporation houses had no picture rails : a picture hook was handed into the People's Story in Edinburgh with an attached note saying:* We couldn't use this when we moved from the Canongate to Prestonfield as there were no picture rails in the houses which could encourage bugs.

SHARED STAIRS AND TOILETS

Strict rotas governed the cleaning of the stair and shared toilet, and women who did not take their turn got a bad reputation. In some tenements a notice was placed over the door knob: 'It's your turn to wash the stairs and passage.' Pat Rogan recalls how relationships with neighbours could deteriorate over cleaning rotas: You had on some stairs house-proud women who were fussy about keeping their stair clean. So if there was a neighbour or two who didn't play their part, they would bring in the sanitary inspector who would serve a notice on them, telling them to get the work done. This caused some friction in some stairs.

Annie Reid remembers using pipe clay to clean the stairs. I was the eldest, so I had to go out when it was our turn to do the stairs. We had to do four doors and a lavvie door. We used whitewash and our pipe clay and rubbed it on the stair. If it wasn't right your Granny used to come out and you had to do it all again. *Sometimes the pipe clay was used to make patterns along the side of the stair. Designs were passed down from mother to daughter. Cathy Lighterness recalls a superstition attached to some of these decorations.* On the outside stair they used to make a half-moon in cardinal red. I only knew one that did a pattern, she did this squiggly pattern. I heard it was to stop the devil, he couldn't find his road in.

As Dodo Keenan of Leith remembers, neighbours would crack down if a family didn't take its turn cleaning the shared toilets. My sister lived in Admiralty Street and there were six families shared one toilet. It was cleaned twice a week. But it all depended on your neighbours. They used to go and send for the Sanitary if someone wasnae doing it. But on the whole they was kept not too bad.

Margaret Thomson grew up in the Calton and Bridgeton Cross area of Glasgow after the Second World War: We had all lived in a single end, but my mum got a room and kitchen – four girls, two boys and my mum and dad. There was an outside toilet and the inside of that toilet it was immaculate, and I know because I often had to clean it. ... [It] just consisted of basically a toilet, no wash hand basin. You would be in the toilet and you could see your friend down the back, because some of the bricks were loose.

Some women like Mary Mackay's mother did not trust the cleanliness of the toilet unless they had scrubbed it themselves. My mother used to scrub the toilet after the next-door neighbours, before we were allowed in. She was always scrubbing it. I used to sit on it wet!

The tenement properties of Edinburgh's Old Town were becoming so run-down by the 1950s that they were virtually impossible to keep clean. Pat Rogan saw many of these houses as part of his duties. Most people strove very hard to keep their places clean. The womenfolk wrought miracles, but they were fighting against very, very heavy odds. ... In the 1950s these properties were deteriorating very, very badly indeed. Superhuman efforts were not enough to maintain them in cleanliness. Broken soil pipes, that was a common occurrence, so when you found a broken pipe, and it was an almost daily occurrence, human faecal matter would be found spewing into a backyard or a front street. All too often the local authority would have to take action because the owners of the property wouldn't have the means to do so.

WASH DAY

The washing machine is possibly one of the most important developments of the twentieth century as far as benefit to women is concerned. Without it, the washing, drying and ironing of a weekly wash was exhausting work which could take days. Margaret Thomson is aware of the difference it has made. You wonder how women managed years ago. When I think of my mother in a two- room and kitchen with six children and a husband. She had no washing machine, no running hot water.

Women generally used to wash on a regular day of the week, as Isa Wilson remembers. My mother used to boil all her washing on a Monday. She used tae wash from early morning till about 4 o'clock. When we came home from school she was washing the kitchen floor and that was everything finished. She used tae wash all the whites and put them on a great big horse. They were beautiful and then, of course they had tae be ironed at night.

35. Agnes Williamson with her son John, carrying a basket of dry laundry, 1933.

Simply heating the water for washing was a major undertaking. Mrs Fairbairn grew up in Leith and remembers gathering wood to heat the water on the kitchen fire: The big iron pot that went on the fireplace was kept in the coal cellar. But it was a whole day getting the water heated, and you didnae burn your coal to heat, it was sticks. You picked up sticks if you could, off of boxes, and this brought the big black washing pot to the boil – all the clothes were boiled in these days, though. And they made up starch, because right round the bed was all white valances. It was Robin's Starch that they got in a packet and they mixed it up and these valances were all starched.

Much of the wash was white – shirts, blouses, night-shirts, under-wear and bed linen. A great value was placed on snowy whiteness and these items were rinsed in Dolly Blue which gave a slightly blue tint and increased the impression of whiteness. When Christina Turnbull was married between the wars she was given a wooden wash tub: It stood in the middle of the floor on a trestle and then the water had to be boiled and emptied into the tub. And a scrubbing-board, even I started my married life with a scrubbing-board. And then the clothes would all have to be boiled, and my mother got the name of being a very good washer. And next the white things were all boiled, then soaked in cold water with a little blue, the 'Dolly Blue', and I think it had a little wooden thing on the top and you swirled that about, you know. And that made them lovely and white.

She goes on to describe the drying arrangements. Clothes were hung out to dry on lines stretched between cast iron poles on the shared back green. Some houses had outside pulleys on wooden T-shaped frames which stretched out from under the kitchen window. Then they had to be hung out on the rope and the ropes went from the window to a big pole away in the back green, a huge pole. Each house had a rope, a 'pulley' as they called it. The women had to stand up and put the rope out the back until they'd used up all their stretch.

If it was raining the clothes would have to be hung in the house. There was a clothes pulley over the fireplace in the kitchen. A string was also tied across the fireplace, as in Bette Stivens' home. My mother had a string across the mantelpiece and on it hung about seven dickeys with wee button-holes down the front. She starched them so you could dance on them and they slipped on underneath the collar – and my Dad got a pure white dickey every morning of his life.

In the first half of the last century, nappies were washed by hand, as Margaret Christie describes: You just had to boil nappies. I soaked them and rubbed them up and down the washing board and then I took them out and rinsed them and rolled them up and put them in a basin and covered them over to soak again and then I boiled them.

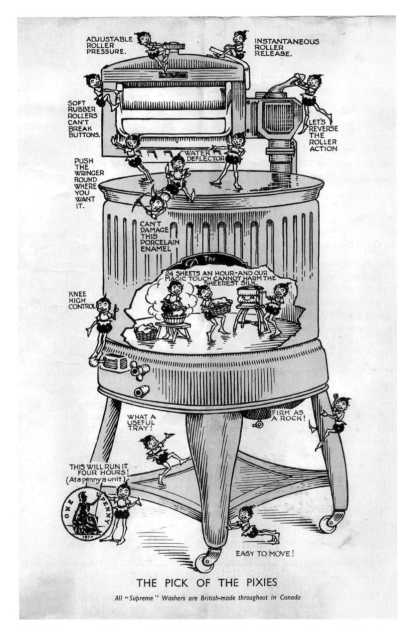

36. The Supreme Princess Model Electric Washer Wringer. Alexander Logie bought one from J. Sibbald & Sons Ltd in Shandwick Place, Edinburgh in 1936 on a hire purchase agreement.

Hire purchase agreements enabled some better-off families to get their own washing machine, like the Logies of Edinburgh who put down a deposit of eighteen shillings and agreed to repayments of £1 a month for eighteen months in 1936 to buy a bright green enamel machine. An alternative was hiring a machine for wash-day, as Bette Stivens did in the 1950s: My first washing machine was on hire. A man came every Tuesday and brought the washing machine in. It was ten shillings and he had a very good business going. He had a whole lot of washing machines and I remember him coming round the doors and he had these long narrow machines. Well he came round and there were six of us living on one pay packet. He would bring it in and plug it in and we would have it for three hours and you got it all done. It was a lot to pay, but we got a lot done.

Joan Williamson managed to buy reconditioned machines. When we moved from the Lawnmarket to Fountainbridge, that's when I got my first vacuum cleaner, it was a reconditioned one, a wee Hoover upright. I got it in the Maitland Radio shop in Lothian Road. They were selling the upright for £35. I got masel' an upright washing machine too, both for £12. I was away with myself.

Once the wash was dry it had to be ironed. In the early years of the century this was done with flat irons heated on the fire. They were used in pairs – one heating on the fire, while the other was being used. Gas and electric irons saved a great deal of work, though Betty Hepburn is another who thinks that labour-saving appliances merely freed up time in which to do more jobs. The extra work I had to do was when I got the gas iron and then the pukka electric iron – that was great, I used to do my entire mum's ironing. You hung the wash on the pulley and when it was dry I did all the ironing and I did all my mother's, it snowballed. The time you had saved you did the stairs or the cutlery drawer.

Many women however were wary of electricity, as was Betty's mother, and were reluctant to use electric irons. This was not just an unwilling- ness to change, but a genuine fear. My mother never had any electric appliances, she still used the gas irons. People were frightened that they would get an electric shock, they didnae know what to do with it. *Margaret McDonald's mother insisted on doing all her washing by hand for the same reason:* My mum was always one who didn't like electricity so we didn't have a washing machine. She did everything by hand, including blankets, I don't know how she didn't have livered-looking hands. She had the old irons as well, I used to be embarrassed when my friends came up because it would be sitting on the cooker heating. It wasn't that long ago, it is only since she moved into Oatlands that she got a washing machine, she still does washing by hand – she's got the old scrubbing board.

THE WASH HOUSE AND THE STEAMIE

Many of the tenements built in Glasgow from the end of the nineteenth century, and a smaller number in Leith and Edinburgh, incorporated wash houses into the building or on the back green or court. This made washing a great deal easier than in a tub in the kitchen. The wash house was shared between the tenants on the stair. Dodo Keenan from Leith describes the procedure: So there was sixteen tenants, an' we had a wash house doon in the basement as well. Number 92 and 94 were the only two stairs in the whole of Albert Street that had the wash house. And, it was only cold water, and you had tae go down first thing in the morning and there was a big boiler in the corner. Now the first thing you did was tae light the fire under the boiler, and get the boiler filled up with cold water. Then by the time you got your washin' down and you maybe done your wee bit shopping, the water was hot, ready to start. Maybe if you got your washing finished by lunchtime somebody would say, 'Could I come in at the

WASH HOUSE CARD.   Tenant No.

Underneath you have a list of the days during which the Washing-House has been set apart for the house you occupy for the ensuing year. You will require to call the previous evening between 7 and 8 o'clock for the key at the tenant whose number precedes yours, and be ready to deliver it over about the same time, on the days stated below, to the tenant whose number follows yours.

N.B.—The Washing-House and Boiler to be cleaned when done.

1931	TENANT No. 1	TENANT No. 2	TENANT No. 3	TENANT No. 4	TENANT No. 5	TENANT No. 6
MAY						
JUNE	8-9 29-30	10-11	15-16	17-18	1-2 22-23	3-4 24-25
JULY	20-21	1-2 22-23	6-7 27-28	8-9 29-30	13-14	15-16
AUG.	10-11 31	12-13	17-18	19-20	3-4 24-25	5-6 26-27
SEPT.	1 21-22	2-3 23-24	7-8 28-29	9-10 30	14-15	16-17
OCT.	12-13	14-15	19-20	1 21-22	5-6 26-27	7-8 28-29
NOV.	2-3 23-24	4-5 25-26	9-10 30	11-12	16-17	18-19
DEC.	14-15	16-17	1 21-22	2-3 23-24	7-8 28-29	9-10 30-31
1932 JAN.	4-5 25-26	6-7 27-28	11-12	13-14	18-19	20-21
FEB.	15-16	17-18	1-2 22-23	3-4 24-25	8-9 29	10-11
MAR.	7-8 28-29	9-10 30-31	14-15	16-17	1 21-22	2-3 23-24
APRIL	18-19	20-21	4-5 25-26	6-7 27-28	11-12	13-14
MAY	9-10 30-31	11-12	16-17	18-19	2-3 23-24	4-5 25-26

Copyright—A. Duncan & Son, 47 South Portland Street, Glasgow.

Ref. 3047   P.T.O

37. A card setting out a rota for using the wash house of a Glasgow tenement.

back o' you?' Thursday was always my mother's washing day. There used tae be a piece of a tree trunk, an' anybody wi' kids, especially in the winter time, they'd sit on that wee tree trunk while their mother wis washin' away. We had a huge back green so we were able tae get our washin' out on the green. Oh I don't think I was ever in the public wash house till after the war finished.

There were usually strict rotas for using the wash house. Sometimes these broke down and led to bitterness on the stair, but good neighbourliness was more common, as Mary Martin in Glasgow remembers. The washing house used to be in the back court. I used the wash house and the elderly women next door used to leave the water and then I'd use it and so on.

An alternative to washing at home was to make use of the Co-op laundry. Women who were loyal to the Store used this facility. Betty Hepburn describes the different services provided after the Second War: I used the Co-op bag wash. You filled up your white bag and they came and collected it. Now you normally got it back the same day, sometimes the next day, and it was wet, so you had to hang it up and do your own ironing. That was about half a crown for that, you got that whole bag full. Then there was the semi-finished bag and you got a book and you filled in each article that you put in there, and they priced it down the side. Now when you got it back it had been washed, and folded and your things were ironed and they were rolled up in brown paper. But then they had another type, that they had the starched finish, you know, if you had the damask cloth, or you wanted something really special, then that was an extra special – you paid extra for that. And then they had a special service for collars. We used to get them in a round cardboard box.

Large public wash houses, called 'steamies' in Glasgow and 'wash houses' in Edinburgh, were built from the end of the nineteenth century by the Corporations of both cities. Here women could have a blether while they were doing their washing, as immortalised in Tony Roper's play 'The Steamie', and this sociability made them an important part of many women's lives. Joan Williamson's affectionate feelings about her Edinburgh wash house are typical. That was the end of hard work for me, I never counted the wash house as hard work. I loved the wash house. I still went to the wash house even though I had my wash-

38. A Glasgow steamie.

ing machine, for curtains and sheets. *In Glasgow, Margaret Thomson had similarly good memories of the steamie.* The steamie was great, you had as much hot water as you needed. You got two hours to do the washing in that time. It was a great way to meet your friends.

Dodo Keenan used to go to the Abbeyhill wash house in Edinburgh after the war. The wash house – oh it was great. I used tae go to

Abbeyhill wash house. If you didn't have an old pram, you got a loan of one. You had your bath sitting on it with soap powder and everything. You got a good washing done there. It was a hot place! You were usually there two or three hours. You'd get a rare blether and hear all the local gossip. You knew everybody that went at that time. It was like going to a club really.

The wash houses opened early so that clothes could be washed in the morning and dried and put away on the same day. Flora MacDonald remembers going before work: I went to the one at Union Street. I used to walk along London Road at 6.00 in the morning with my pram. You would go before work. If you hadn't much washing you got done by 7.30. It cost 6d when I first went.

Many women like Agnes Elder liked to get the wash done before the children went to school: Oh it was handy. I could get down the road and back for the bairns going off to school. I could be hame for quarter past, twenty past eight. Get the bairns up and get them across the road to the school. Then your house got done and your ironing got done.

Even with the steamie, doing the wash was still great deal of work, as Elizabeth Dawn, living in on the South Side of Glasgow remembers: It was tubs with a boiler beside them. You just pulled a big wooden crate up to your waist. You would wheel it up and put your washing in and you'd put your coloured washing somewhere and put your whites in first and then throw in the coloured and then put them in the trolley soaking wet and let them drip. After that you took them to a drier and dried them, if they were half dried you took them home and hung them out for the air. It was a lot of work then.

Some of the wash houses had a crêche. Mabel Dawson remembers the one at Abbeyhill: The children were in a wee ante-room with a person looking after them, with toys – you paid extra – from two or three years old. Or you would leave the children at home with a neighbour.

The wash house made washing easier and women like Joan Williamson would take washing for their family. Even though there was just my husband and daughter and myself, I was still washing for seven, because I washed for my mother and my dad and my brother and my sister. You wouldn't go to the wash house without asking your mother if she had anything, you made it lighter for her.

Jessie Campbell, who used the wash house at Abbeyhill, Edinburgh, sums up women's fond memories of these places. She was active in the demonstrations against closure in the 1960s. There was no way you could wash these things in the house. You couldn't get a washin' done not like towels, sheets, anything big, so the wash house was handy and you could make as much mess in the wash house as you liked and use as much water as you liked 'cos the answer to a clean wash is the rinsing. If you went with your rollers in, your hair would come out lovely. That's why you see lots o' women in thae photographs with headscarves on and rollers in. The steam used to make your hair great. There was a good atmosphere in the wash house, very friendly. There was no trouble. Everybody helped one another. You didn't have to ask to have a fold, you just went over and automatically everybody just mucked in. There was one day when I went to the wash house when a woman came in with a sore back and she was told to stand aside and all the other women got stuck into her washing. If they opened the wash house again I'd be down there today. It wasn't for the want of us trying to save it: we tried but it wasn't a success.

8

For Better, for Worse

You had to tolerate it. It was different if you were deep in love with him. It was different if you didn't feel that way.

Marriage for many offered the opportunity to embark on an adult life free from parental control. Yet the realities of married life could be very different from the romantic ideals of young couples. Women could soon find themselves responsible for the welfare of a young family with very little money coming in to the home, and, if they were unlucky, a man who drank away a large proportion of his pay, or abused his dominant position in the household. Roles were very clearly defined and it was hard for a woman to break out of them to take control of her life. In such circumstances in particular the support networks of family and neighbours were crucially important to women.

'A GOOD MAN'

The happiness of a marriage depended to a great extent on whether a woman, like Elizabeth Smith, had a good man. Olivia Wilson considers, I was lucky, I had a good marriage. *Liz Kent also remembers a long and happy marriage:* We got married in the Hogmanay, and we never looked back a' these years. I always hoped to be lucky, I never missed oot on anything. Just the one man for sixty-two years. *Councillor Davidson too loved and respected his partner.* I was married in 1930 to a wonderful woman. She died in 1985 and had she lived we would have celebrated our Golden Wedding – fifty years with the right woman.

Betty Laing is perhaps typical of many who acknowledge problems but feel that all in all she had a good marriage. We have had our ups and downs. We have had a lot of deaths and tragedies in the family, his side more than mine really, but on the whole it has been a good life. We haven't went into debt or anything.

Money was the focus of many difficulties in marriage. Most men took their responsibilities as bread winner seriously, but it was fairly unusual

123

and a matter of great pride for Mary Holligan and her husband that he handed over his unopened pay packet on pay day: There weren't many like Dennis, he never touched his pay envelope. As he used to say, 'The man that takes money from the pay envelope steals from his family.'

Bette Stivens remarks on the very general prejudice against married women going out to work, which did not begin to weaken until the 1960s. This left them trapped in economic dependence. Of course you couldn't go back to work after you were married. Even if you were hard up, the last thing was to go back to work. It was not the done thing. Oh no, in these days the man was supposed to be the provider. It was ridiculous if you look back – there was no liberation.

Fathers, like Betty Hepburn's, were not expected to do anything towards running the house and family, though they would generally contribute in other ways. My dad started work at 7 o'clock and came home at 7 o'clock at night. He was really, really tired. He did repair work, no housework at all. He painted and he was great at that stippling on the doors. He mended our shoes on an iron last.

General social convention gave the man the whip hand in a relationship. As Mary Hutchison puts it, Of course men were more masterful then, you know: 'I am the master of the house'. *Undoubtedly there were women in unhappy marriages who had to suffer in silence when a man demanded 'his rights'. As Marion McIntosh remarks, once you were married sex was something* You had to get used to ... that was it. *Or as Mary Blackie says,* You had to tolerate it. It was different if you were deep in love with him. It was different if you didn't feel that way.

Bette Stivens points out how times have changed: in the past men lost face if they helped with housework or children. There's more come and go with a husband and wife than there used to be. Husbands will do more now. They wouldn't wheel a pram or carry a bag of messages in the old days.

NEIGHBOURS

What made life livable for many women in less satisfactory marriages was the support offered by other women – family members and neighbours, as we see throughout this book. Although life for many women in the first half of the last century was very hard, tenement living itself

39. A group of women and their children gather for a blether in the Canongate, Edinburgh, about 1910. Snowy white aprons were a matter of pride.

was conducive to neighbourliness. Everyone knew everyone else on the stair and the level of trust was such that house doors were usually kept unlocked. Living close to family or in-laws meant that many young women could feel that they were constantly being judged on the way they ran their house and family, but the support of an extended family was invaluable. Shared values also meant that the communities policed themselves to a great extent. There was a genuine feeling of comradeship, which was essential for survival in such difficult conditions, and many people have experienced a strong sense of loss over its disappearance.

This feeling is eloquently expressed by Dolly Conroy, who grew up in Govan in the 1920s. In the old days, up the tenement close ye just came out yer door and ye met Mrs So-and-So coming out as well, and ye blah blah blah blah and that was it, everything was so different in those days. Up a close, you're talking about eleven families up one close, so therefore you see you were in more contact with them. Oh neighbours were neighbours in those days. Yes, ye never shut yer door, yer door was always open and the same key done the whole of the close sort o' thing. Especially in Govan, in my young days all the doors of the stair had the same 'check'. And then ye never really locked yer door in those days, which is not the case now. They were good days those days; neighbours were close, oh yes, very very close.

Neighbours provided an essential support system in times of trouble: women would help each other out by producing food, watching children, helping with chores or lending money. There seems to be a general consensus that this neighbourliness disappeared when the old communities were broken up. Mary McPhater, born in 1912, grew up in the Maryhill area of Glasgow: I was thirty-two years in Rolland Street. It didn't matter when you went out or when you came in, you always saw a neighbour and they always spoke to you. If the kids were not well, or you wanted a message, there was always somebody there to see to you. I think there's something in a tenement building that's homely because you had neighbours you could run to. Now where I am in Knightswood, sometimes you never see a soul.

This sense of comradeship was missed so much by Joan Williamson's mother, when they were rehoused to the Gorgie area of Edinburgh, that she moved the family back into the centre of town: The 1920s saw a big move by the Edinburgh Corporation to build lots of houses for families who were overcrowded. My mother had applied for a house in the early Thirties: there was seven children in our family, three boys and four girls, but by the time our name came up two of the eldest brothers were married. We lived at that time in Newport Street [Tollcross] in a room-and-kitchen with outside toilet shared with another three families, so you can imagine how we felt when we heard we were moving to a three bedroom house, living room, kitchenette and bathroom in Gorgie Road, right opposite Saughton Park ... Mum had never settled in the house, she missed the town and all her friends, so because of that she decided to get an exchange. We moved back in 1941 to a room and kitchen with gaslight and outside toilet. The house was never empty, we were back to where we started!

Sandra Speedie remembers tenement neighbourliness in Glasgow: When I was young and living in the Calton there was always a neighbour popping in and your mum would say 'Have a wee cup o' tea' and even in Buchazie you know somebody would come to the door. Ye lived up the tenement, you were out sweeping the stair and somebody would come up with their messages and you'd say 'Och leave that bag there before you go up the three stairs, and come in and have a cup of tea'. But I don't think people have the time to do that now.

TIME OFF AND OUTINGS

Life was not all grim, despite the incessant hard work. The wireless or radio was important entertainment for women at home – though they would usually be doing something useful at the same time, as Mima Belford says: You never sat in and did nothing. You were never idle. You'd be sitting knitting, sewing, crocheting or something.

While men would often spend evenings out, many people like John Sinclair remember sociable family occasions: A favourite night for staying in was Sunday night with the family to play cards. I went out every night bar a Sunday. But on Sunday the family, and maybe the next-door neighbours, would come in to play cards. Newmarket, Whist, Rummy, Solo, Old Maid: it would end up as a sing-song of course. You'd get bored and someone would start to sing. Though you'd still be playing cards. There's be the odd screw-top – but only for the men. There wouldnae be whisky.

40. After her children had grown up Ruth Fraser took up cleaning work. In 1949 she was working in the Regal Cinema, Edinburgh and took her husband Robert and daughter Joan on the works outing to Whitley Bay.

There were also impromptu gatherings with friends and relations at which families made their own entertainment. Betty Hepburn remembers: You would learn party pieces from your parents' parties when you were allowed to stay up a bit late.

New Year in particular was a special occasion, despite the hard work of getting the house spotless to enter the New Year, as these Edinburgh woman remember. The women would get everything just so-so. and the last thing I always done, maybe ten o'clock at night was wash the stair and then come up and have a bath and get dressed. And the ashes were always emptied out at quarter to twelve – like the Old Year going out. *New Year was a common time for seeing relations.* My mother always used to have a pot of soup because our relations used to come from Stenhouse to Stevenson where we lived after twelve o'clock. Every time they came in after they got their drink they got a hot bowl of soup to heat them up.

Married women who were not working outside the home might miss out on some of the trips organised by workplaces. Betty Hepburn remembers annual trips when she was working at the Co-op in Edinburgh. The work took us: the Store. We always had one trip. And if there was anything like that on [the Glasgow Empire Exhibition in 1938] they used to run a bus. I remember going back to Glasgow and going round a lot of the museums. I remember going to Whitley Bay and Berwick.

There was no entitlement to paid holidays until after the war. There was time off in July – Trades Weeks in Edinburgh followed by Fair Fort-night in Glasgow – but that often did not amount to anything, as Greta Connor remembers. Trades, in the beginning when I began to work, wisnae much because you didn't get paid for it. It was just unpaid leave. So unless you were a saving person and you'd laid by for it, it was nothing to look forward to.

In Glasgow in particular all but the poorest families would try to get out of the polluted city at least once a year: 'fresh air fortnights' were encouraged by local government and welfare organisations. Day trips to Edinburgh were common, but the favourite outing was 'doon the watter', whether by steamboat or train, to the resorts of Largs or Dunnoon or the Isle of Bute. Vast numbers left the city together during the Glasgow Trades and Rita Gentle remembers the crowds at Central Station: The queues were unbelievable – half way down Argyle Street. Everyone

41. Sailing down the Clyde, c.1950.

was going doon the watter. The queues were horrendous, full of greetin' weans and laughing weans. *The steamboats were a very fondly remembered part of Glasgow holidays, though as George Telfer recalls :* Nine times out of ten it was raining. We were washed out and washed back. *People could live very cheaply at the coast as they often took all their provisions including pots and pans with them. It was not uncommon for whole streets to go away together. These invasions were often regarded with suspicion by locals, as May Hutton recalls:* The landlord sat at the outside toilets guarding his chickens because he thought that all of the people from Glasgow were going to kill his chickens and eat them. No way would the girls go into that toilet so we used a bucket in the bedroom.

In Edinburgh Betty Hepburn remembers street picnics organised by the mothers in Gorgie. Two bus loads would go on a Sunday morning. Someone would just say 'Do you think we should have a picnic?' Yes, aye, that would be good!' You'd take all your own food, but they'd organise the bus. We'd all pile in, mums, dads, uncles, the lot. The mothers got the games organised. You were always organised for a game, you were never left to wander. Skipping ropes would come out, swings from the trees.

LEITH HOSPITAL DAY
JUNE 12 1920

42. Devlin's Trawler float on the Leith Hospital Day Pageant, June 1920.
The Royal Infirmary of Edinburgh and the Leith Hospital fundraising
pageants provided an entertaining family day out.

*Some places had traditional outings – like the Leith Carters' Trip which
Mima Belford remembers from the horse-drawn cart days.* I went on
them because my sister's husband worked in the docks and he got
us tickets. You all piled on the carts and they actually placed you. It
was marvellous how they got you all on it. Then it used to be Dalkeith
Park you went. A horse and cart drawn by a big Clydesdale horse
and the men all polished the brasses before you went. The horses
got prizes for being the best dressed. Then you'd away out to Dalkeith
and have a picnic and races and everything. Then they'd take you
back.

*People turned out for the procession of the Carter's Trip even if they
didn't go on it, as Mrs Gardiner remembers.* This was a big procession
round the foot of Leith Walk, all dressed up with bonnets and things,
you know, and went away perhaps to the station and took the train
away to Glasgow or away some otherwhere like that. And the procession met them at the station and brought them home again or

the band turned out and all the folk turned out and everything. Anybody that liked could go and dress up and dance in front of the band and everything like that, and then everybody turned out to see it, you know. It was an occasion.

James Stuart Grahame, born in 1906, thinks women contributed in a big way to the Leith Pageant, another well-remembered family day out. Every year it was an annual event, they had what ye call the Leith Hospital Pageant. And a' the horses were a' dressed up and the lorries were painted specially for the occasion. And the lassies, ken, the lassies had mair enthusiasm than laddies, I also think the lassies have more initiative ... I used to think that the lassies used tae take a particularly interested part, oh wi' their tambourines, dresses and motors a' done up ... And it used tae be great and they used tae collect money fir Leith Hospital.

WOMEN'S GROUPS

Women also had more organised self-help systems. The generally important role of the Co-op is discussed in the next chapter, but the Scottish Co-operative Women's Guilds deserve mention here as an example of women banding together to support each other. As Nan Sutherland says: The Guild was worthwhile joining because we all really helped each other and we knew each other, how we were placed financially, things like that. And really we had a good Guild, and I always say no matter what you ask the Guilds for you'll get it. You will never be let down by a Women's Guild, Co-operative Women's Guild.

There were Guilds spread across Scotland. Edinburgh's first two branches opened in 1896, and growth was steady. As Nan explains many new local branches, like the one in Gorgie were opened. They got so big that they branched out ... when I joined in '41 the membership was 354. That was the membership of Gorgie Guild. and if you were wanting a position you had to have a waiting list even for committee for tea members, for tea makers and things like that. You had to have waiting list because the women were all anxious to work, all anxious to put their heart and soul in the Guild.

The guilds had both a social and an educational purpose, helping to expand understanding of various issues, as Mary Hutchison attests: It was a great education for the women. If I had never joined into the

43. Banner for the Carmyle branch of the Co-operative Women's Guild, Glasgow, c.1920.

Women's Guild I would have had a much poorer life.

They were popular as offering women a chance to go out by them-selves, when there was little other entertainment available. As Cathy Gay points out, Their husbands wouldn't object to them going to the Women's Guild: they were all other women. *Going out to meetings did depend on husbands being willing to be left alone, or to look after the children. Not all were as co-operative as Mary Hutchison's husband:* We've had a few arguments about it at times, especially when I had to go out oftener. But on the whole I must say I was a very lucky person where that was concerned, being able to go. But of course when I came home at night I had to tell him all about it. *He would look after the children provided they were in bed early:* He wouldn't want to be bothered with them running about the place. But they should be in their bed anyway, he said. He was very strict.

A similar organisation was the Women's Section of the Labour Party to which Ella Williamson's step-mother went. They met once a week and she was on the committee and helped to make the tea and that sort of thing. ... They had speakers, discussions ... they used to have a social evening on a Saturday night and my father used to play his accordion for the music.

DRINKING

Poverty, with the consequences of poor health and housing, was the biggest single problem facing women within their marriages. Drink and violence too often accompanied this kind of life. The brunt of keeping things together fell upon the women. It was their sacrifices which kept families fed, when men could seem selfishly ready to indulge themselves at the pub. Alex Kellock says: I never saw my mother eat. She never ate with us. If I asked her she would always say, 'Oh! I've had mine already'. If you think about it with a family of eleven children – well twelve, as one died – you needed a dozen eggs just to give everyone one egg. My father wasn't a bad man but he did sometimes leave her short and he did tend to drink.

Drinking was a regular habit among working men. Molly M. of Glasgow recalls: A lot of men in the street were coming in drunk but you never saw my dad like that, my mother wouldn't tolerate it.

Helen Nickerson remembers the scenes when her father, a fisherman, returned home to find that her mother had taken an advance against her husband's wages while he was at sea. He would get in such a state ... When he used to come in he'd have a drink in him and he used to stand her in a corner and then clear the table and then he'd go out and get drunk. He broke the dishes ... he went mad ... but he never, ever lifted his hands to anybody.

Some women had to try and catch their men on pay day if there was a risk that the money would be spent down at the pub or betting shop, forcing a spiral of pawning, poverty and hunger, as Margaret McDonald remembers. Women had to meet their men at the factory gates to collect their wages before they went to the pub. It depended on the man, usually his wife got what was left of his wage after he had been in the pub. *George Flannigan from Edinburgh recalled how in the 1930s women used to gather outside the pubs to wait for the wages: they would never go in.* Saturday was the big day. There was no such thing as a Friday pay. The womenfolk used to gather outside and wait on the menfolk coming out.

Men drank close to where they lived in the old tenements of Glasgow and Edinburgh, which had the advantage of making husbands easy to find. After the slum clearances and the move to the peripheral housing schemes like Easterhouse in Glasgow and Westerhailes in Edinburgh women found it much harder to get into town to chase the wages, bundling the children into prams and having to change buses en route.

Women could be driven to despair. Cecilia Russell recalled a story about a hard drinking dock-worker in Glasgow in the early years of the twentieth century. One of them went home on the Saturday afternoon, drunk of course, that was nothing unusual. Anyway his wife told him that she was going to throw herself in the Clyde. He said, 'Wait a minute.' She replied, 'There's no use in coming. You can't stop me!' He said, 'Stop ye, be damned. At the foot of the road there's a seven foot fence an' ye'll no' be able to go over without help, so I'll come and help ye ower!'

A few women also went to the pub – though as William Thomson of Leith suggested, if a woman went into the men's bar, she got chased out. Oh aye, not now of course, but then. Oh right out. *The jug bar of a pub was where alcohol could be bought and taken away, as Alexander Dunnet says:* You only seen women in the jug bar. That was a wee place for them. That wis a'. They didnae go intae the bar. To the jug bar that was it.

Dodo Keenan's mother used to go regularly to the pub – though she was a puntilious church attender too: My mother always took a drink. ... I don't mean she sat in the pub all night – maybe at 9.30, before the pub shut, she would be in for her nip and her half pint. That was every night. I was the youngest of fourteen and many's the pub I've stood outside. She always liked her bit tipple and when she got a handbag, she used to like a handbag that could either carry her hymnbook and her bible or half a bottle. And she could go on a Saturday night and she always had some friends that she could meet. And she could come home on a Saturday night and we often wondered how she got home. She never missed church on a Sunday.

However it was widely considered unrespectable for women to drink. Those who wanted to avoid the jug bar for this reason might buy drink in from the local store. They were thus forced into the role of secret drinkers, whilst social drinking among men was accepted. Nancy Strathie remembers the common condemnation by other women of those who went to pubs: A lot of them scoffed at women who went into pubs. They would buy the drink from the licensed grocer. I mind in Buchanan Street, this woman used to go in with a jug and I used to think that was terrible – an old woman going in for a jug of beer. You ken, used to say, 'Fancy that, oh here's someone come in wi' her jug, ken. 'Cos our mothers were good living people you know.

Women were responsible for the moral and religious welfare of their children within the home, and their judgements would reinforce gender roles and respectability. Beth K., who grew up in Bridgeton in Glasgow, remembers her grandmother's anger when her grandfather, a miner and fisherman in Dysart, Fife, took her with her brother for the rare treat of a bottle of ginger and a packet of crisps. She was only taken to sit outside the pub once. My granny was Old Kirk and god-fearing, and strongly disapproved of drink and was furious and shocked that Grandad had taken us near a den of iniquity. I do remember the smell of beer as the doors opened and same smell on Grandad's breath. It was exciting. That was the only time. He never took me on his boat though. That was men only.

The Temperance Movement had its first roots in the West of Scotland in the nineteenth century as an attempt to combat the serious social problem of heavy drinking. Thousands of leaflets and tracts were distributed by the various societies, but more important were the many activities that were organised as counter-attractions to the pub – meetings, social evenings, choirs and so on. Juvenile sections were developed to educate children against the evils of alcohol. Bert Keppie, born in Edinburgh in 1924 joined the Good Templars when he was seven. It was a good friend of my mother's, she was a Good Templar herself because her father had been a real alcoholic, who knocked his wife and family about a bit. She had joined as a young woman and eventually she was running the Edina Juvenile Lodge of Good Templars in Rygo Street. They met once a week and had little concerts and you were encouraged to recite and sing and there was an annual competition in Edinburgh.

Tearooms flourished during this time of temperance sentiment and were an important recourse for treats as women could enter them quite freely. They were a particularly distinctive part of Glasgow life, though Miss Cranston's famous suites of tea rooms, designed by Charles Rennie Mackintosh, were out of range of most tenement dwellers. Between the wars countless other tearooms, like City Bakeries in Glasgow and Patrick Thomson's, known as PT's, in Edinburgh were popular.

DOMESTIC VIOLENCE

A certain amount of violence between men and women was common-place in the tenements, particularly in the single ends of the Old Town in Edinburgh and the overcrowded East End of Glasgow. Occasional violence would not have drawn much comment. In a culture in which children were commonly physically punished, adults under stress would some-times lash out against their partners.

Glasgow Councillor Davidson, born in 1909, remembers the first time he went canvassing for the ILP in Water Street, Cowcaddens, where it took the heart of a lion to go into at all. My father knocked the door and an angry voice roared out, 'I'll be with you, stay where you are.' So my father gently pushed me back down the stairs a little, the door flew open and a man appeared in the door with a towel over one arm and an open razor in the other – raised! He said 'I'm sorry mister, I thought you were my brother-in-law.' My father was not a very big man but he was full of courage and he said, 'Well lad, I'm glad I'm not your brother-in-law: as much as for your sake than mine I'm glad, but whatever is wrong you are not going to solve it with that. Close the razor.' The youngish man did. So we went into the house and he explained the circumstances. He was shaving, getting ready to go out and his wife was getting a bit weary of him going out all the time and she had protested and finally he said, 'I smacked her in the gub, so she had went up the stairs to get her brother.'

The problem was exacerbated by poverty and alcohol, and in some relationships abuse became endemic. While hen-pecked husbands were known it was women, conditioned to defer to the man as the master of the household, who were almost always the victims. The money spent on drink was the cause of many arguments on pay day, and women and children often feared the return of their drunken husband or father. Joan Williamson of Edinburgh remembers the family hiding from her father. Saturday was worse 'cos that was always the pay day. I can remember if my dad was sober on a Saturday we'd go for a walk. But if he came in with a drink on a Saturday early on that was it. Nobody went anywhere. And many a night rather than argue my mother would kid on she was away out and shut the door. He never found her hiding place yet, in all these years she used to stand at the back of the curtain in the room until she thought he was sleeping, then she used to come in beside us. He would be in the kitchen of course, in the bed. He never struck us but he could be different with my mother. We used to take off and stand in one of the stairs in Morrison Street, hiding from him. He would come in with the place in darkness, you'd be in your bed, but you'd not be sleeping. You knew what was going to come with the arguing. He would count all the heads. My older sister, she was my mother's back up. She was a teenager by this time and if an argument got too much she'd get us dressed and get us out.

Violence in the home was for some women an expected part of married life and it inevitably involved or was witnessed by children. P. McG., from Glasgow, witnessed domestic violence from an early age and shows how it was repeated in families. She herself was later involved in a violent and abusive relationship. My dad used to hit my mum about a bit and they had been married for twenty-eight years, but you were never allowed to say a bad word against my dad, you know. My granda' was also violent towards my gran. That was my dad's father, his mother's second husband, and he worked on docks and he used to come in on a Friday night and my gran would have soup and everything all ready. I don't know how much they shared in those days but he'd put £2 in and go out with £4. My gran would never say a word to him and that was every night. He'd come in for his meal and go back out again. My dad kind of went through that as well as he had three older sisters. My dad's three sisters done everything for him till he got married. My dad was twenty-one and my mum was seventeen and that was just the way it went. My da' was just like my granda'.

Women with young children had few choices but to stay in a loveless or even violent marriage. Mary Blackie, born before the First World War, used to hide out in the stair and then climb in the window once her violent drunken husband had gone to bed. For her intimidation and violence was also sexual. Until the 1990s it was not an offence to rape your wife. He wouldn't let you sleep. He used to come in at all hours in the morning and I always knew when he was coming in and I had to get his tea on, and if he was drunk and you were dying to go back to sleep and he wouldn't let you. He kept bashing you on the back of the head. If you had a headache it didn't make any difference to him. You still had to have intercourse. The only time that I had freedom from him was when he died in 1973, because I had to be in the house for him to get his dinner and you would have to have intercourse at odd times. I had forty-seven years in fear. ... I would bring his breakfast into his bedside and he would lift it up and throw it down the pan. My family used to ask why I stuck it, I stuck it for them. Nobody would take you in.

Mary did run away from her husband but was not able to take her son with her. One day I ran out of the house and I was living in a place where I had to do the stairs at Kelvinbridge for the sake of getting the room and he sent word through my sister that he was putting the boy in a home. *Mary eventually went back to her husband. Some, like this Glasgow woman finally found the courage to leave the marital home, despite the disapproval and inevitable poverty entailed, when their children began to be affected either emotionally or physically.* I was married for two years before I had my son but then I didn't want to leave because of him. I took it for so long and eventually I left because I cam' home one day and my four year old son was locked in by himself.

Until later in the twentieth century people subscribed to the general attitude that marriage was for life, and 'you have made your bed and now you must lie on it'. There were few places that women could go with children and in small communities no safe houses where an angry partner would not find them. Women who did not stay with their husbands often felt that in failing at marriage they had failed to fit into society and to be a proper woman. Divorce at this period was unusual and a social stigma. Not all broken marriages ended this way: some women, especially Catholics, lived entirely separate lives whilst still legally married. Elizabeth Dawn from Glasgow left her marriage to a man who was a womanizer, although he was never violent. I was seventy-three years married and I was only seventeen years with him.

For Mary Blackie things seem very different for young women today. See the young ones that are married now, they have the time of their lives. They are the boss now. The women are the bosses.

9

For Richer, for Poorer

Well like everybody else we were hard up, but like
everybody else we were all in the same boat.

*As part of the work of running the home, a woman became the main
money manager. This involved juggling demands on very limited funds
and it was particularly difficult when times were hard, especially in the
depression between the wars, when many families were forced to fall
back on unemployment benefit and Parish Relief. A variety of strategies
were used to make ends meet, but many women had a deep fear of debt.
Families lived on the edge and survival often depended upon women pull-
ing off miraculous feats of managing. Jane Patterson, a medical social
worker in Edinburgh's Old Town after the Second World War, explains
the pressures:* Very often the woman had to be the brains of the
concern. He made the money, but it was regarded as a matter of
particular pride on the woman's part if the husband handed her
his unopened pay-packet. There were really two standards. One
was what did the husband earn; and what do you receive? Which
were totally different things. You see, the husband had his pints on
the way home and his betting and one thing and another, and
many women really didn't receive enough to feed and clothe their
families, pay the rent, pay the gas, pay the electricity.

MAKING ENDS MEET

*The example of weekly expenditure from 1913 given in the appendix on
p.186 demonstrates how tight the finances could be. This budget amounts
to 31s 11d, against the father's wages of 32 shillings. Only one penny
is allowed for contingency and none for saving. If the husband was out of
work or handed over less money to his wife, she would have to manage
on what she had. The woman who runs the budget of 1913 gives her
husband 1s 6d pocket money for his drinks and betting. Credit was usually not an option – Isa Keith like many remembers:* ma mother had a
right horror o' debt.

Some like Ella Williamson got control of the family wage: Oh I got the pay packet. I think it was the done thing. The men were quite happy to hand it over to their wives. As long as the wives could manage, it was all right. *Others weren't so lucky: Mary Blackie, whose husband worked on the docks in Glasgow, got housekeeping money entirely at her husband's discretion.* I couldn't get a loan of five bob off him. When the kiddies' half crown benefit came in he took that off your wages. In fact I got a daily wage and if there were no boats up there was no money.

If wages were given in cash the woman often didn't know exactly what her husband had earned, and she had no way of compelling him to hand money over. Joan Williamson tells of her mother's strategy for shaming her father. They never got pay packets in these days. They used to get their wages in their hand. And you were lucky if you got this without a cut. And on this particular time he said he had some money, but she knew that he had more. He flaked out and went to sleep and she went through his pockets. My dad he was a riding master and groom at the stables and he used to hide his money, but anyhow my mother found it. And she got his shirt tail and put his money in his shirt tail, she got a bit of string and tied it in a big knot and left his shirt to put on in the morning. And when he got up in the morning, he never said a word about the knots. This was her way to let him know that she knew he had money.

In Leith many men worked on the trawlers and would be away at sea for maybe two or three weeks. Charlie Beskow remembers how hard it was for his mother to manage between the wars. Well, when my father was at sea, my mother never drew any wages until my father's ship docked on the other side and the skipper wired through to the firm, in case there were any discrepancies, and anything had to be taken off his pay ... She'd be down at the shipping office every morning till they got word. She got a chitty then she went to the post office, or a bank and drew the money. Then it was a burst, but for three weeks you'd be on a hunger.

It was normally possible for the wife to get an advance on her husband's wages while he was at sea, sometimes to the man's fury, as Helen Nickerson recalls: We used to have to go doon for a sub, when his boat just left the pier, from the Company for to keep us. My mother would have no money, so the result was that she had to send us,

44. A sewing machine could provide a valuable way for women to augment the family income without having to leave the house.

Jenny, doon for a sub off my father's wages afore he even earned them. And when my Dad used to come in my mother used to say to him she'd lifted two pounds, and then she would send Jenny to run efter him and tell him she'd lifted five, because he would get in such a state, because he'd hardly have any wages to come hame to.

As we saw in chapter 2, children often contributed to the household budget by doing odd jobs. Once they left school and began earning they were expected to hand over the bulk of their money. Dodo Keenan started work in Duncan's Chocolate Factory in Leith in 1935: I started keeping myself at sixteen on sixteen and six [16s 6d], that was my wage. My mother got ten shillings and I got six and eight [6s 8d] back. That was for clothes, shoes, everything.

Another strategy for supplementing the family income was to take in a lodger, as Cathy Gay's mother did between the wars: Believe it or not, we lived in a room-and-kitchen and she took in a lodger in the room and we lived in the kitchen until I was five.

In times of dire poverty people had to resort to whatever they could to provide food and heat. Meg Berrington went beach-combing in Leith as a child: I remember going down to the beach which was down at

Black Grounds, and collect coal and bits of wood, because our parents didn't have enough money to buy coal for the fire. We used to do that when we were young, not all the time, but at certain times we had to do this.

If people didn't have money to pay the rent they could just up and leave, beginning a cycle that was hard to break. Annie Anderson remembers these moonlight flits in Newhaven. I think the rent was five shillings or six shillings. Yes, they collected it each week, but luckily my mother was always lucky enough to have it. We knew people that didnae – there was an awful lot of moonlight flittings in these days. You could get a house today and get another one tomorrow, when we were young.

WORKING WOMEN

Despite the critical levels of income on which most families survived at this period, the general prejudice against women going out to work after marriage was very strong. Betty Hepburn worked for the Co-operative in Edinburgh just after the Second World War, and puts it clearly: I was in the St Cuthbert's bakery then, up Morningside, and then I was there for about eight or nine months and then I got married, and I left then. You had to, you were more-or-less, not forced exactly, but when you married you left, it was the done thing to leave when you got married ... It wasn't down in any contract, really, that you had to leave. But those days your husband didn't like you to go out to work, I mean, that was dreadful if you had to go out to work – apart from illness, I had to do it later. When you got married you were supposed to be in the house. Everybody did it.

Some women went out to work once the children were older, but this usually met with the husband's disapproval, whatever their economic circumstances, as Mrs Gardiner, born in 1882, testifies. I didnae want to work after I got married and ma husband didnae want me tae work. I did go and get a job though, when the children were off ma hands. An' I went an' got a job, cleanin', cleanin'. So I came hame an' told ma husband. He was mad, flamin' mad! ... He says 'What'll the men in the boat say aboot ma wife goin' oot tae work?' I says 'You ask the men if they'll come an' pay the rent.' An' I says 'It's honest work and I'm not goin' tae get intae debt and beholden tae anyone. I'm too proud for that, to beg an' borrow.'

However some women, like Thomas Hare's wife in Leith between the wars, took on casual work to meet a special need: My wife never worked. Occasionally she would come down when the waitress in Baltic Street was on her holiday: she worked in her job for about six months, till we got tae accumulate a little bit o' money tae buy some furniture, because ye had very little money then.

Cleaning and laundry work were the usual areas where married women found work, like Mrs Fairbairn's mother in Edinburgh. She was a charlady, a charwoman, and she worked for the ladies that had more money than us. My mother would go out and work for a whole day for two and sixpence [2s 6d] for the spring-cleaning ... to wash all the white woodwork and then they'd washing to do, ironing to do. It was away out at Marchmont and Morningside that people wanted people to clean, so you had your bus fares off that as well.

Another way to make some extra money was to take in work, usually washing or mangling. Dodo Keenan's mother did this to earn some money for her own use. Oh, if you had seen our back green wi' washin', she was a great one for washin'. There wis, eh, the wee paper shop

45. A woman selling from a barrow on a Saturday evening, on the corner of Virginia Street and Argyle Street, Glasgow, c.1950.

across the road from us – it wis a mother an' daughter that were in it, an' the mother was crippled with arthritis. Ma mother did the washin' every week for her. But she always made a wee bit money on the side. Well, she couldnae go in an' have her nip an' half pint every night if she didnae. ... An' she used tae say, 'It's ma own money I'm drinkin'.'

A licence was required by anyone wishing to trade at the Barras and Briggait markets in Glasgow, but many would run the risk of being caught by the police for selling things without one. Molly M. remembers going with her brothers and her parents round the Briggait: My dad made toys and bits of furniture and my mother made odds and ends for dolls' prams. And so it kept us going and we didn't let anyone know our business, she kept herself to herself. It was the Briggait we used more than the Barras – the Barras was upmarket a wee bit if you know what I mean. Folk are still going to the Briggait the day as they did a way back, and keep the bundles in the lane. I mean I done it myself, I done what my ma done. We spent money on a bunker to stow our stuff, but it's the same idea the day as it was a way back years ago and they still lift them the day with the Paddy wagon and take all the bundles away and you got fined.

The fishwives of Newhaven in North Edinburgh were a fiercely independent breed of women. There was no stigma attached to their selling the fish caught by their husbands and fathers in the way their mothers and grandmothers had done before them. Elsie Tierney's mother was one such. Well, the fish market was only at the bottom of the close where we stayed and Ma used to go down there about half past six in the morning. Then Ma used to come up back home and she'd get me up to get me ready for school and we took maybe our breakfast together. She used to go out again, and she'd go down, pick up her creel and her skull, pick up the fish at the market and then she'd get on the tram.

Apart from the perceived slight on the husband, the main barrier to married women going out to work was childcare. There were a small number of early nurseries in different parts of Edinburgh and Glasgow, set up to look after children whose mothers had no alternative but to work. Mary Tolbain's mother had to go out to work after her father died: My father died in 1909 and my mother went out to work. She

46. An Edinburgh Corporation day nursery, Dumbiedykes Road, 1924. Such nurseries provided day care for working mothers.

cleaned the Bank of Scotland. In the mornin' she'd be away oot, she'd leave us. The two youngest, we were put into the day nursery in Stockbridge, I mind that. I mind cryin', I didnae like to go. It was a matter of coppers. She would leave us and then come and fetch us after she finished. There was a lot of children there.

It was more usual to make use of grandparents. In the 1920s Cathy Gay's mother worked cooking, making lunches in a bar – a pub – and at three o'clock after school I went to my grandmother's who fortunately lived fairly close. *While many women could rely on their family to help out, Dodo Keenan's mother had other ideas when Dodo wanted to work during the Second World War.* It was only during wartime when the women started goin' out to work. My mother wouldn't watch ma kids. She said she'd brought up fourteen of her own, she had never done it for the rest of the family and she wouldn't do it for me. When he was on leave, she wouldn't even watch them tae let us go out.

Some women solved the problem by working shifts when the children were at school or during the night. Bette Stivens managed this as a nurse after the Second World War. As far as I'm concerned I would never allow my children to become latch key children. ... I had to find a shift or a Sister nice enough to give me a shift, where I could be at home when my children came home. When they took their dinners at school, which I did not like, I could work a bit longer then, because they were away from half past eight in the morning to half past four. Very often I did night duty, in the nursing, so that when I got the children off to school I went to bed and was up for them when they came in at half past four. I didn't mind starting early in the morning, because my husband would get the children ready for school and then I would be home for them coming out of school. I liked it when I took the very early shift or the very late shift. At the weekend my husband had the Saturday and Sunday off so I could do anything then.

Betty Hepburn went back to work part-time at the Co-op in 1962 when her husband became ill. My husband was ill for many, many, many years before he died and I just had to go out to work. I had to fit in work that would suit looking after the children and seeing to him, just doing everything. I went back to the drapers actually, it was the drapers that used to take on the part-timers, at Bread Street. And at Christmas time, of course, you got work at Christmas time, it was quite good.

Attitudes to married women working changed sharply during the Second World War, as Norrie Campbell points out: Married women were expected to go out to work to fill the places of the girls who had been called up for the women's services, munitions or the Land Army. Later they had to register – my mother registered, but was not expected to go as my brother was too young to be left at home.

Propaganda urged women back into the home after the war, and most if not all were happy to comply. Ella Williamson worked at an Edinburgh fishmonger's before and after she was married, but stopped when she could after the war. He asked me to come back during the war, after I wis married like, but I went and worked for him and then when I was having Betty I had to stop working. And then after I had Betty he came and asked me back to the shop again. So mother watched the baby and I went back to work till Alec came out the

Army, which was 1945. I stopped working as soon as my husband came back. ... I didnae want to go out to work. I know a lot of women, they had got the extra money and they weren't going to go back to the old way of working, they were kicking at the traces. You cannae blame some of them, where their husbands kept them short of money and that, they were getting a good wage.

Although attitudes were slowly beginning to change, Bette Stivens's deliberate decision to continue her work as a nurse after the war was made in the face of her husband's disapproval. From when they were tiny my children accepted me working, but my husband never accepted it. He thought a woman's place was in the home – the original chauvinist pig! He hated it, he did everything to get me to stop. I worked because I was ambitious for my family to be well educated. All mothers want their children to be better than what they were. I didn't spend very much of the money I earned on myself. We used to argue about it. He never said 'You're not working any more and that's that', but he used to moan and groan about it. 'A woman used to be able to manage on her husband's salary'. I used to understand it, it was a sort of a slight on him, it wasn't the proper thing to do.

THE STORE

Membership of the Co-operative Movement, which was very strong in the first half of the century, was a fundamental part of the way many women managed to make ends meet and even to save a little for special needs. For a minimum joining fee of one shilling, a person received a share number and Store Book. Every purchase was then written down in the book. If a child was sent for a message they gave their mother's number, and the check they brought home was placed on a spike until it could be later added to the book. This is why so many men and women can remember their mother's Store number. The book was usually paid up at the end of the week. The Society's profits were distributed to members in the form of a dividend on purchases, paid out each quarter.

Many people, like Betty Hepburn, shopped almost nowhere else: You did all your shopping – you did all your groceries, all your butcher meat, all your milk, you got your tokens, you know, latterly, to give to the milkman. You did everything in the Store in those days actually, that was your main focal point. *Greta Connor can clearly remem-*

47. Women clerks processing checks to work out the dividend at the St Cuthbert's Co-op check office, 92 Fountainbridge Edinburgh, c.1952.

ber how her mother dealt with the family finances in the mid 1930s. It was a ritual on a Friday ... The rent money was laid by, coal money, so many coppers for the gas, your club money which covered the clothing and pennies for the insurance – maybe only sixpence [6d] for the whole family. But that was religiously put away. What was left, she had managed to get herself a Store Book. She had about £20, an enormous amount of money. I don't know how she acquired that, maybe someone in the family was good to her. So what was left was put in the Store Book and you could deal on that up to £7 or £8 and then at the end of the week she would pay what she could. Maybe next week she would clear it if she was a wee bit lucky.

A person could not spend unlimited amounts during the week. A sum had to be left in as security and this varied over time. Dodo Keenan explains: For every £1 you had in you were allowed to use up to sixteen shillings in the Store. They'd write it in your book and the book got handed in to the desk. They made it up to see what you'd spend in a week. You could go to the butcher's, the baker's, the grocer's, the drapery. If you spent £5 you could just pay £4 that week if you were hard up. My mother used to say 'Always have your Store Book and you'll never be in debt.' At one time, just before the war, St Cuthbert's paid dividend of four and twopence [4s 2d] in the pound.

For some women the dividend was crucial, as Nan Sutherland recalls: There was lots of things you could do with your dividend. It was really a ... it was God's blessing all the time. And when you shopped nowhere else we always had a good dividend, always had a good dividend because my money went in the Co-op.

Betty Hepburn remembers Divi Day: It was a day out actually. I remember chumming my mum for her, and you always got taken out somewhere, maybe for a cup of tea somewhere. It was really special. Or you got extra sweets or we had an extra special tea at home. I mean that's money, money! But it really was something, dividend time. You could either ... withdraw it all, leave some of it in, or leave it all in if you wanted, for a later time. Most people got their rent paid through I think their Store dividend at that time. You always tried to put extra into your share account at dividend time. You'd have to build it up a little bit if you were needing something out with maybe somebody getting married.

For special events like weddings or maybe for clothes women could take out a 'club' with the Store: You got this club, depending what you borrowed. I think if you borrowed £10 you got it for twenty weeks – you got twenty weeks to pay what you borrowed in weekly instalments, and you could use your club. You could spend that money as soon as you got your club out. I think we all bought furniture and clothes and everything off a club. I think everyone had clubs. Twenty pounds was the normal, in my time.

It wasn't just the Store that organised 'clubs'. Here Isa Keith describes a menage, which could be arranged on a stair basis or by a group at work. The word comes from the French ménager – to save, or handle carefully. When we grew up and got working, in work there'd be girls that had run a sort of similar type o' thing, what we would call a menage. And they'd have say ten of you and you'd put two shillings a week and that would probably buy a pair o' shoes. And you picked a number, you picked the first week and somebody else would pick the second and whatever. And what the girl did, she'd go round and collect all the two shillingses and hand it tae the one and she'd go along tae the shoe shop and buy the shoes 'cos she had the money. And everybody had their turn and of course the shop got the money, they werenae in debt.

The Store also encouraged children to save by issuing a Penny Savings Bank, as Betty Hepburn recalls: The Penny Savings Bank was a steel tin you could get the children to put the pennies in, if they went messages for other people. And they used to love having one of them because you could save up and it was a wee surprise when it was opened. You took it down to the shop: you didn't open it, you didn't have the key for it. The Store kept the key for it so you had to take it down and they opened it and, of course your eyes would pop, you know, when you saw how much you had collected. ... We had one and we used to take it down at New Year time for to buy the New Year goodies, and then the next time would probably be about holiday time, so that gave you extra for your holidays.

THE BUROO AND THE PARISH

The world slump of 1929-31 and the subsequent depression in the economy was keenly felt in Scotland. The alarming rise in unemployment had a devastating effect on the standard of living of the poorest families. Unemployment benefit or 'the Buroo' (from 'Bureau'), was administered by the Labour Exchange and was available for a limited time after the loss of a job. John Preston from Leith remembers the inadequacy of the amount paid: See people hadnae nothing. When you think a man an' a wife an' three bairns – twenty-seven shillings in the old money on the Buroo, that was frae there. Sixteen shillings for the man, eight shillings for the wife and a shilling for each kid – that's all you got, a shilling.

During this period many women like Meg Berrington's mother worked to supplement their husband's benefit, but had to keep quiet about it: My mother went out for a bit once a week, this was in between having children as well, doing washing. She worked for a doctor, up Ferry

Road. She got five shillings for doing that all day. She did the washing in his house. A lot of the mothers did this to get a bit extra money, but then they had to be careful of the Buroo, because you weren't supposed to be earning any money because the father was on the Buroo.

During the depression some firms would lay workers off every alternate week. If they were under eighteen they had to go to day school, as Dodo Keenan recalls. I went to Torphichen Street [Edinburgh] to Buroo School, and that was when I worked in Duncan's and sometimes they had a quiet spell and you were put on one week workin', and the week you wernae workin' you'd to go to Buroo school. You go to lessons, maybe cookin'. On a Friday we had to go up to St Giles Street to get our money.

Once unemployment benefit was exhausted the next stage was to apply for Parish Relief, known simply as 'the Parish'. The Means Test introduced in 1931 to assess such claims became a hated, degrading procedure. The income of all members of the family was taken into account. Greta Connor's memories are bitter: It broke up families, because as soon as a child became of age to work [14] and was lucky enough to land a job, he either kept them all, or he had to leave the house. The ones that hadnae a job, to get benefit, they'd go to the Buroo School and you had to go in every day to qualify.

It was often felt as a stigma for a man to be kept by his working children, as Helen Nickerson recalls of her father: It used to be the Parish then, ... and they put him on the Means Test. When we started work and we had to keep him and her, my dad resented that because he said he never would live off his family and then he went oot and tried and went and got a boat. But I mean jobs were hard to come by even in those days, on trawlers.

Robert Noble, born in 1917, recalls a visit to the office in Edinburgh: When my father died, mother was left wi' seven of us, we had to claim from the Parish Relief. Well, you had to go up to Johnston Terrace. Well, there was no money coming in – the insurance was nothing because it was only penny and tuppenny policies, you know, that's what we paid. So mother was in being interviewed with this man for to get Parish Relief, and he was giving her a lot of cheek. 'You're an able-bodied woman – why don't you go out and work for your family?' Well, my oldest sister, she was sitting outside, waiting on mother coming out, ... so she goes in and she says, 'Ma mother has a kid o' three weeks old', she says, 'she has to be breast-fed so often a day, that's why she cannae work.' But there was nothing done about it.

The worst memory about the Means Test was that someone would come to the house and assess a family's possessions, as Mima Belford describes. If you were comfortable he'd point to something and say 'You can do without that'. Bits of furniture or things you didn't use every day. What they called 'luxury'. *This happened to an old lady Betty Hepburn knew.* Your place had to be really threadbare. I remember an old lady on our stair and she had a rug in front of the fire and he came and told her to sell it.

Bette Stivens was nine when the man from the Parish visited her home. My mum couldn't get any money at all. I remember the man coming – he was absolutely horrible. I remember hanging on to my mother and being quite upset, so was she. This would be 1926 and my mother asked for money and the man said she could sell her piano. So that's when she went out to work because that was the last straw.

There would be strategies for getting round the man from the Parish. If they knew he was coming, possessions could be put next door out of the way. As Molly M. of Glasgow remembers even the entertaining of relations was frowned on. They called it the Parish Day and my mother's sister would be away in to visit her and the guy from the Parish came up ... If they caught someone else in the house they would want to know who it was and 'how could you manage to give them a cup of tea if you were asking for money from the parish'. My mother would look through the keyhole to see who it was and my auntie would go into the room out the road. You'd hear old people saying 'the parish days are back again'.

As part of the system of Parish Relief the Police handed out boots and clothing to needy families like Mary MacKay's: You could get free clothes from the Police, shoes and stockings. It was called the Parish. I remember the corduroy trousers, you went to the Police in the High Street to get them. We had to wear them because we needed them. The stockings were so rough they scratched my legs.

The boots were easily recognisable and Mabel Dawson of Edinburgh describes the resulting stigma. I wore Police boots. My father was unemployed so my mother took us up and got boots. I was the eldest of six, see. They were old-fashioned and had holes punched in them at the ankles. You were looked down on. 'Polis Boots!' was the cry. People knew right away you were hard up, but you wore them: you had to. *The holes punched in the ankles were to identify them, as Leither John Watt explains:* Well I remember we went up tae the High Street wi' ma dad, five o' us, an' we got policemen's boots. Policemen's boots, they were a' tacketed, a' studded. There was five holes on it, five holes on the ankle bit, 'Do-Not-Pawn-These-Boots'.

THE PAWN

Before the Second World War a pawnshop could be found on almost every corner in areas of Edinburgh and Glasgow. Goods were exchanged for cash and a ticket which had to be produced when they were redeemed within a given time. Molly M. describes the regular pawning that raised a little extra cash for the week. Say it's a Monday morning, there was a queue at the pawn, it was the father's suit – not the woman's gear, it was always the father's suit because the woman didn't have any. She was that busy bringing up the weans and she didn't have good clothes. The man of the house always had a good suit, so the suit was always looked after, given a wee press with brown paper and then back into the pawn on a Monday, lifted on a Friday for them finishing their work on a Friday because the man like to go out on a Friday night or Saturday so they would put on their suit and their collar and tie. If you were Catholic you wore it on a Sunday for chapel. It was a yo-yo, it went in on a Monday and out on a Friday, the shoes as well. Their shoes, a wee bundle went into the same wee box. A lot of them men didn't know that their suit went into the pawn, as it had to be there on a Friday.

Even though everyone was hard up, some still felt a stigma about being seen going into a pawnshop, as did Margaret Thomson: Now that I didn't like, I wouldn't go. Everybody went but I was always frightened in case someone saw me. They would say 'But why is it bothering you – you will see them and they will see you, everybody does it, it is your own stuff you are actually pawning'.

The 'shilling a week man' used to sell clothes, linens and blankets around the doors. Val Smith here describes a common strategy: You've

got to really have been there to realise it. People were really poor in those days. You used to have these clubmen that came round the doors. Say you would pay two and six [2s 6d] a week you could get blankets and stuff. If you had nothing in the house to eat, it was a godsend for the pawn. That gave you something to pawn. It was for the sake of putting something on the table. The minute they were out of the door you wrapped the stuff in newspaper and you were off to the pawn. And then the trouble started when the man came back on Friday for the money. 'Tell him your mother's not in.' That was the favourite saying. And you would go to the door and say to the man 'My mother's not in.' Your mother would be hiding behind the door.

Nancy Strathie remembers her mother's view on this common practice. My mother managed, you know, but I mean in the olden days you used to see them all – a lot o' people buying clothes, sheets and that from the shillin' a week man, an' goin' up the pawn an' pawnin' them. ... Well my mother never did that, but my mother always said, better doin' that than goin' out stealin', because you still had to pay the goods up, you know. An' then – you put them in and then if you wanted 'em back again you'd to pay the money you'd been paid. *Of course if you sold on the pawn ticket you couldn't claim the goods back. Elsie Tierney remembers benefiting from this.* People would buy things new and not even take them out the wrapper and they used to pawn them and sell the ticket – all my Witney blankets came out the pawn shop and they were still in their wrappers.

Helen Nickerson remembers her mother pawning things in desperation to buy food for the children. We were that poor ... I can always mind when we used to have to go to the Salvation Army for to go for the breakfast in the morning for porridge when my faither wisnae working. We even used to go to the school sometime withoot any breakfast and my mother used to pawn a parcel to run and gie us a piece through the school at playtime for us. A pair o' sheets or something that she would maybe hae taken on frae some man come to the door ... for the sake o' making extra money for us, for something to eat. We had nae shoes, we never used to wear shoes in the summer.

48. Opposite: A woman taking a bundle to a Glasgow pawnshop, 1930s.

MAKING DO

When times were hard women were thankful for what they could get from other people. Mrs Fairbairn remembers the handouts that her mother received from the people for whom she cleaned. My mother got cast off clothin' if the people had children, and maybe sometimes it was shoes. That was a big item to get. But sometimes they were too small and sometimes they were too big, but you still had to wear them, because they were good, leather you know.

Women were resourceful about making and altering clothing, as William Drever remembers of his mother: And, being one of a big family of course my mother used to make all our clothes. You know, she made trousers, jackets, the lot, out of suits she got from people she used to work for. You know, she did so many hours' cleaning for half-a-crown [2s 6d], a day's washing for half-a-crown, and if the man of the house was throwing out a suit, the bottom half from there [the knee] down would be in reasonable condition – the cloth. She would rip it all up and actually remake it, not just cut it. ... When you think about what she used to do, it was really fantastic.

These 'new' clothes were not always comfortable but were better than the 'parish clothes' as Molly M. describes: She made trousers out of old coats, you know, the boys' trousers and they used to have scurves round their legs, so she started putting a wee bit velvet on it, you know, to take off the scurves. The jerseys she used to knit, she knitted the jerseys and all that. And the jerseys that they gave to the boys to wear were rough and the shirts were grey and they were really rough and the boys came out in boils all round their neck.

Cathy Gay hated the look of made-down clothes: It was quite a poverty-stricken life, really, although I never wanted for anything basic, but I remember my aunt's coat would be made down to fit me. A woman did this for us for about five shillings – made down these coats. ... They sometimes had fur round the neck and to me they looked home-made and I hated them. I recall being so hard up, having to buy one stocking at a time – I think it was Barnet's who sold stockings in ones – at sixpence per leg! They were a shiny artificial silk.

49. A group of children from Albion Place, Leith, 1920s. Some of them are wearing coats that are too big for them. Coats were sometimes cut down for children or remade into trousers.

Mary Gilchrist became a mother during the Second World War when the practice of make-do-and-mend was essential, and clothes would go round several families. She attests once again the importance of women supporting each other. Well like everybody else we were hard up, but like everybody else we were all in the same boat. Everybody was hard up and things were still rationed, but everybody helped everybody else, and we all helped each other. If you had a good recipe for something that didnae use an awful lot of fat or sugar you passed it round, or if your child had outgrew something you passed it round too. It might go round two or three families, and everybody recognised it, sometimes you got it back. We just took the elastic oot the legs of romper suits, and made them into dresses. And old shirts, when the collar goes we got it and by the time you got the shirt it would be minus a tail, because the tail had been used to put a new collar on. But these two wee lassies had dresses made out of shirts.

The generosity of the poor was what kept many women afloat in the hardest times. When everyone was in the same situation, there was help for someone even worse off, as Jenny Wilson recalls: Well, you didnae think it was hard, I mean, lookin' back it's hard, but at the time you never thought it was a hard life. Then, you see, everybody was the same. I mean, there wasnae any 'keepin' up with the Joneses' in they days. If your mother had thruppence and your next-door neighbour had nothin', she'd gi'e her three ha'pence.

10

In Sickness and in Health

It only took one person to fall ill, or a child to fall ill
and people rallied round.

*Given the circumstances in which people lived, illness was an almost
inevitable part of life in the tenements. As Greta Connor succinctly puts
it:* Bad health was caused by poor housing, insanitary living conditions, poor diet from lack of funds and an inbred feeling of inferiority which these conditions gave you.

*There was a great knowledge of home remedies among tenement women,
which could be used to cure minor ailments. 'Wise women' in the community were often the first port of call when illness struck. It was only
in extreme cases that the doctor was called, as before the establishment
of the National Health Service in 1948 the cost was often far more than
the family could afford. However during the first half of the century
acute infectious diseases – diphtheria, scarlet fever, meningitis and consumption – were common and the fear of infection and death was never
far away.*

SIMPLE HELP

*It was in times of illness that the mutual support network of tenement
women came into its own. As Pat Rogan said of the tenements he knew
in Edinburgh:* It only took one person to fall ill, or a child to fall ill
and people rallied round. Neighbours would look after sick children
and look after the other children in your home, so you had the
freedom to go to the hospital. The community feeling was absolutely wonderful and people were generous in everything they did.

*Poor nutrition was a fundamental cause of ill health among the poorest: the practical charity remembered by Walter Smith in Leith was
effective in the simplest way.* An old lady, who had a shop in St
Andrew's Street – this old lady used to cook about six or seven
sheep's heads, bags o' vegetables, an' make a beautiful soup. She
used to cook it in a great big iron tub and she used to cook this

159

every Saturday night for the children on Sunday morning. The children used to come down an' get a lovely plate o' soup, on a Sunday dinnertime. *Mary MacKay's mother gave similarly basic help to her neighbour:* My mother always had a pot of soup on, and poor as we were, she used to bring the little kids in from next door – they had thirteen of a family.

Support in times of illness was often expressed by gifts of food, as Mary Blackie of Glasgow remembers. In Anderston people all lived in single ends or rooms-and-kitchens and if anybody was ill somebody would hand in a plate of soup or slices of bread.

Neighbours would also look after the children if a woman was giving birth, or a member of the family was ill, as Betty Hepburn remembers. The rest of them on the stairs would say, send Jeanie to me, or Johnny to me, and Catherine looked after the kids till it was all over, because they didnae have room. They would be sent to neighbours – 'Oh come and stay with me'. It was just another in the bed. *Isa Flucker remembers staying with a neighbour when her brother was ill:* My brother that's next to me, he was very ill when he was young. He had double pneumonia, and they couldnae move him, and my mother had to get a neighbour to put our bed into her room to let us sleep there so my brother could get the room to himself.

Some newer residents in a community could find life very hard until they got to know the neighbours. This member of a multicultural elderly care centre is the oldest sister in a large family and remembers arriving in Glasgow soon after the Second World War when she was thirteen: We did not know anyone, and with my mother in hospital and my father at work every day, I ran the house. I got the children ready for school, cut their hair, did everything, because we did not know anyone. I did not know how to cook so a neighbour taught me how to cook. My mother was in hospital for about eight months.

As Molly M. of Glasgow shows, reliance on family, who usually lived close, kept people from the poorhouse or charitable institutions. If you were desperate I daresay you could have used the St Vincent de Paul [Charity]. I can't honestly say I saw my mother doing anything like that, because she had my granny who she could fall back on and she had sisters, so I think they sort of helped each other.

HOME REMEDIES

Simple ailments were dealt with at home: Mary Holligan's mother had a large repertoire of home cures. If we had toothache, the coarse salt, which was placed on a shovel, then the shovel was placed on the fire and heated and when the salt was hot it was poured into a sock, usually one of my father's black ones. So you held it to your jaw hoping it would help to burst the abscess. My mother's favourite cure for all ills was one half cupful of Epsom salts: she held it until you gulped it over, she was ready with a spoonful of jam which one had to swallow immediately, but it seemed to do the trick. For colds we got ipecacuanha wine, syrup of squills and glycerine, mixed, which seemed to help.

If my mother found us scratching our heads out came the Rankin's ointment or if it were finished, she would soak our hair in paraffin oil which, to my mind, made the situation worse; one couldn't get rid of the smell for days. If one got a 'line' from the school doctor you had to go home alone, as one was treated like a leper. When I was very young and found I had a tooth that hurt, I was sent round to Granny Howden's who promptly, with her fingers, pulled it out. She did this for me quite often.

50. Labels for two popular home cures which could be bought from the chemist, 1920s. Such remedies were widely relied upon before the advent of the NHS.

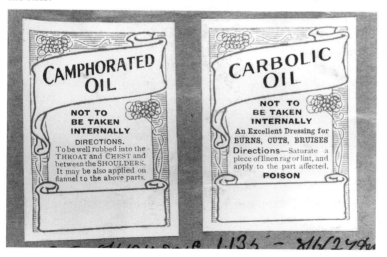

Poor diet meant that many people suffered, as Marald Grant of the Guild of Aid in Glasgow recalls, from very bad teeth – terrible teeth, and a lot our applications for aid were for dentures. *A sock filled with hot salt for toothache was on Dodo Keenan's list of remedies:* For colds camphorated oil and emulsion and sometimes thermogen wool. Chemical food for a tonic; soap and sugar poultice when something got festered or the need for inflammation drawn out. Father's sock filled with hot coarse salt for toothache. My first iron when I was married was electric, that was in 1937 – then you got a piece of brown paper, you soaked it with vinegar and ironed it and put it on your chest or your back. It did the trick.

Poultices were popular to treat colds and bad chests. Madge Earl re-members Bread poultice mixed with grated soap made up with boil-ing water, put into a cloth, squeezed out and put on your chest. It was cheap. *Bette Stivens's family remedies included a hot toddy:* Other home remedies included a half onion carried round in the back pocket for rheumatism; and sulphur and treacle for constipation. A cure-all was a hot toddy heated with a hot poker.

Some women, like Christina Turnbull's mother, became known for special knowledge of cures for common ailments, and were key figures in the community: People would come to my mother and ask for advice or, if she would mix up a poultice for them or their husband, if there was anything on the chest. There was no National Health Service and people didn't have the money to pay for a doctor. I mean young people nowadays, and the not so young, have just no idea what like it was. Everything had to be paid for, and now they go to the doctor if they have a cold or the child has a cold – then, you just had to do your own medication. If you fell and skinned your knee and it festered, you got hot bread poultice on, white bread, and just as hot as you could bear it on. There seemed to be an awful lot of gumboils with children. They'd come to school and their face would be all wrapped up. And earache, there seemed to be an awful lot of earache too. An awful lot had to have their teeth out – people just didn't bother about toothpaste, just didn't do it. They used to suffer real agonies with toothache. There wasn't even aspirins, ye just had to suffer it. They would put something hot on their ear, a woollen sock was one thing: hold salt over the fire till it was hot and then put that in the sock.

For Betty Hepburn there was a granny on the stair who used herbal remedies. Where we stayed there was an old lady and if the normal cures from the chemist weren't helping your mum would say 'Run and get Granny Love'. She'd get what we called the witch's pot. I'm sure it was herbs she used. She never charged for this.

Bette Stivens underlines the importance of the chemist – anything to avoid doctors and hospital, which people feared, not only for the cost. Your chemist in those days was as good as your doctor and more so, because you hadn't the money to go to the doctor. The chemist was your best friend. People were frightened to go into hospital, there was not very much hygiene. People didn't want to get the doctor even when they were seriously ill, apart from the payment, 'cos they were frightened they would be put into hospital. Even the Royal Infirmary, sixty years ago, once you go in there you'll never come out.

DOCTORS AND DISPENSARIES

If the illness was beyond cure at home, the doctor was called. In the 1920s, the standard charge was two shillings and sixpence (2s 6d). By the late 1930s this had risen to seven shillings and six pence (7s 6d). As an alternative people sometimes went to dispensaries. The two

51. The baby clinic at Grove Street Dispensary, Edinburgh, about 1920.

described here by Jean Hay were attached to hospitals in the centre of Edinburgh. If you turned ill and you had to go to the doctors you had to pay half a crown [2s 6d]. So you used to go to the out-patients at the Chalmers or Deaconess. That was free. They called them Dispensaries and charity paid for them.

Some people were able to take out a form of health insurance with one of the large national Friendly Societies, such as the Loyal Order of Ancient Shepherds or the Independent Order of Rechabites. These societies developed in the nineteenth century and provided members with un-employment and sickness benefits and funeral expenses. Elsie Tierney's mother worked as a fishwife. I belonged to the Free Fishermen's Society for the hardship and sick benefit. We didn't get the doctor free, because my mother paid him in fish. *Another Friendly Society was the Ancient Order of Foresters, which Margaret Cullinan joined.* When I started working shortly before the National Health Service, I was told to join a friendly society for the benefits, Edinburgh Corporation told me to join. My father was a member, so he advised me to join the Foresters. *Norrie Campbell also belonged to the Ancient Order of Foresters.* For dental services and spectacles you would get this through the Foresters. We paid 5d a month I think, and if you were ill, they would send you on a convalescence for a fortnight.

There were some doctors who waived charges: Marald Grant of the Guild of Aid recalls one such. Dr Mitchell, a very well-known lady doctor on the South Side of Glasgow, came and was our doctor for nothing, for anybody that needed anything. She came once a week when we had our babies in the nursery.

Joan Croal remembers that the advent of the National Health Service, which gave free access to medical treatment, was a relief for doctors as well as patients. I remember a doctor friend of mine in 1939, she was a paediatrician, she had just qualified and it was her first call out. And she got called to see this baby and it had measles. She was very worried about it and said to the mother, 'I think I should come back tonight', and the mother said 'Oh no' and she in her innocence she just thought that the woman was trying to save her the trouble of coming out. Then she realised that it was because she couldn't afford to pay for another visit. So she said 'Oh no, I'll just come and I'll not charge you'. When the

52. Hawthorne Brae Convalescent Home for Tired Mothers, at Duddingston, near Edinburgh, 1920s, run by the Edinburgh Medical Mission to give respite to women from the most overcrowded areas of the city.

National Health came in she said what a relief for the doctors 'cos they didn't have to worry about that and they could concentrate on the job.

Greta Connor remembers her first visit to a doctor under the NHS: After the National Health I went and introduced myself to the doctor and found he was just an ordinary kind of person you could sit and talk to. Before you had to look in your purse and see if you had seven and six [7s 6d] first.

However, for many the doctor was still only called in times of severe illness. In an attempt to break down these barriers against healthcare, the Edinburgh Medical Missionary Society began a service 'For the medical, social and spiritual benefit of the people of the Cowgate and for their own training in preparation for medical missionary work.' The 'Coogate Doctors' ran daily surgeries, paediatric, gynaecological, antenatal and dental clinics, two dispensaries, and a domiciliary service. Jane Patterson was based at the Cowgate Dispensary in the 1950s as a Medical Social Worker: I think a lot of these people tended to have a complete dislike of anybody that they saw in an authoritarian position. They would rather go to the old grandmother and ask about the baby's feeding and so forth. At the time I'm speaking of, the beginning of the National Health Service, all doctors were authority figures. Probably I was too. They saw you as educated and therefore an authoritative person. Sanitary facilities were appalling ... Yet there was barely a patient who came to see the doctor to be examined, who had not taken the trouble to get thoroughly washed and have clean underwear on. This was obviously something that you did if you were going to the doctor, no matter how difficult or how inadequate the facilities were, and sometimes the doctor remarked on that, you know, that she was beautifully turned out – clean clothes and all the rest of it.

The Society also ran the Home for Tired Mothers at Duddingston, established in 1894, to provide immensely beneficial convalescent breaks for worn out mothers and sickly children. As a response to poor housing in the Cowgate area they also opened a club for patients in the 1950s: Now this was on the same lines as the 'Peckham Experiment', where the sort of club facilities are available for patients who were having medical care, because the housing was so poor that nobody could really entertain in their own home. They came to the Dispensary to entertain, to meet their friends, and to have parties etc, and that was one night a week, a Tuesday evening.

Glasgow health workers, the 'Green Ladies' who were both feared and respected, made a very important contribution to gradually improving health standards in the city's poorer areas. Norma M., who was a Green Lady in the 1950s, stresses that We had no right of entry. If we went to a door and the person answering did not want to let us in then that was the matter closed. Funnily enough that was extremely rare. *She goes on to describe the status accorded to these invaluable women:* We were respected and accepted as being a very important part of the community. And it was all trams then of course and the tram driver if they saw you in the road would stop, and it didn't matter whether it was a stop or not; and the conductor would offer to take your bags, you know give us a ride to the next, 'Where are you going nurse?' Anything at night, whenever you had to go out at night you were never scared about going because you knew you were perfectly safe. And men would come up and offer to carry your bag at two in the morning, if they happened to be passing. You never had the slightest worry about it. If you were in uniform you were OK.

INFECTIOUS DISEASES

In the first half of the twentieth century infectious diseases could spread like lightning through a tenement. There had been an outbreak of deadly flu immediately after the First World War. Diphtheria, scarlet fever and pulmonary tuberculosis (TB, also known as consumption) were all fatal diseases. Children were particularly susceptible to certain diseases. At the beginning of the twentieth century one child in five died before the age of one year. The mortality figures per 100,000 of the Scottish population as a whole between 1901 and 1910 were: tuberculosis 209; respiratory diseases 277; scarlet fever 9; whooping cough 44; diphtheria and croup 17; and measles 34. The improvements that took place in the early part of the century had a marked effect as can be seen in the figures for 1931-9: tuberculosis 77; respiratory diseases 172; scarlet fever 4; whooping cough 11; diphtheria and croup 9; and measles 9.[1] These figures are for Scotland as a whole and were much higher for Edinburgh and Glasgow. The incidence of infectious disease increased directly with the overcrowding and poor sanitary conditions found in the most densely populated areas of both cities.

An outbreak of smallpox in 1894 led to the establishment in Edinburgh of a fever hospital in Colinton: there were several such outbreaks in the early years of the twentieth century. Mrs Gardiner remembers the smallpox in Leith in 1894. There was a time of the smallpox, when

53. As part of the campaign against TB during the 1950s badges were given out to those who partook in the mass X-ray programme.

1. M.W. Flinn (ed.), *Scottish Population History from the Seventeenth Century to the 1930s*, Cambridge 1977, pp 398-9.

I was just at school. I lived through that, we never took it. They were all marked, their faces all marked you see. They were all eaten away by the disease, it was terrible. They were taken away and some of them died of it and some of them would have been better dead to tell the truth, because their faces were so disfigured.

Glasgow had the highest mortality rate in the country from tuberculosis, which did not fall to below 100 deaths per 100,000 until 1950.[2] It was eventually brought under control after the Second World War with the introduction of vaccines and antibiotics, the pasteurisation of milk and mass X-ray campaigns. Dodo Keenan remembers the fear of it. Consumption was the disease you really dreaded. You seldom recovered. It was caused by housing conditions or milk. Once you fell for it, the whole lot fell, because they all lived so closely confined. Where I lived, once one got it the ambulance was never away, either. TB, the fever, pneumonia or diphtheria, and they didn't seem to have a cure for it. Up to seventeen or twenty [years of age], if you got TB that was you!

Jane Patterson saw many TB cases in her work: Oh yes, TB was just always there. At the very beginning of my time in Edinburgh, people were waiting anything up to eighteen months for a sanatorium bed, and sometimes they were put into little huts in the grounds of the TB hospitals and really in isolation. You know, they were there by themselves. ... But there still was quite a bit of sending to Switzerland, and of course the discovery of certain drugs to assist in the treatment of tuberculosis made a tremendous difference.

Crowded housing was a key issue in relation to TB. The medical profession particularly disliked the use of curtains around the bed recess, as they reduced ventilation around the bed. Barbara Anderson recalls a visit from the doctor: We did have a bed recess, with curtains, but one day the doctor came in and sat down and he pulled them down and he said 'Don't put them back', so I didn't. I think Helen had measles or something. *Pat Rogan, local councillor for Holyrood in the 1950s, recalls the rehousing implications:* TB was a terrible scourge at that time; it was number one priority, pulmonary TB in particular. One reason was that disease spread so rapidly in a family. If you had two or three children in the house, you had top priority. You went ahead of everybody. So once somebody had TB the medical officer he would

2. Public Health Department Annual Reports 1900-1950.

54. Fresh air was considered crucial to fighting disease: nurses and children outside at Robroyston Hospital, Glasgow, April 1926.

say, 'Get them a new house straightaway', no matter who else was pushed back, they were given priority.

TB was so widespread that in Glasgow whole housing schemes were infected, as Margaret Cruickshank remembers: My brother-in-law died of TB in the house we moved to ... Sugarhill in Govan they called it, and it was a TB scheme, every second house had TB then. Now it is demolished, there is only one or two houses left. *This member of Focal Point Community Centre in Glasgow remembers:* I was only in mine two days when someone stopped me in the street to say 'Do you think you will like it here?' and I said, 'I'm sure I will', and she said, 'The old lady didn't because her daughter died of TB in that house'. I was only two days in with very young children at the time. I immediately sent out for the Health Board and they got the place fumigated. I felt a bit happier then.

Before the war both scarlet fever and diphtheria were notifiable diseases which had to be reported to the Sanitary Department. There were epidemics of scarlet fever during the first quarter of the century, which had a serious effect on children. Many who survived the acute illness suffered later from crippling heart disease. Diphtheria was known as 'putrid sore throat' and in many cases proved fatal. It was brought under control by the national campaign for immunisation, launched in 1940. Mrs Jamieson of Leith lost her brother: James died of diphtheria in 1924. They took a swab of the throat and the doctor came back and said it was negative. But he grew worse that night, and mother says the doctor said, 'I don't care, this child has diphtheria', and he wrapped him up and took him in his own car. It was Doctor Walker in Wellington Place. Oh he was a gem – he was a real family doctor. And I don't know if it was one or two days after it, the police were at the door – James was dead. You see there was nothing then, the throat just closed up, there was no injections, nothing like that.

With both diphtheria and scarlet fever children were isolated in hospital and allowed no visitors, which could be devastating for mother and child. Annie McKay remembers being in hospital in Edinburgh: I was in the City Hospital with diphtheria when I was four. I got fair worried at three o'clock: the sister would open the doors and say 'That's your parcels Annie'. You'd start to cry because you weren't allowed visitors. The parcels would just come in the wagon. But when you got that bit better you got right to the barrier and my mother would stand there. It was sad to think you couldn't get in touch with your own people. I used to lie flat on my back, no pillow or nothing. *Patients were allocated a number, which appeared in the local paper, as Betty Hepburn recalls.* If you got scarlet fever you were taken normally to Colinton Hospital. You were isolated; your parents weren't allowed in to see you. Every night there was a report in the *News* and you had a number and it told you if they were improving or getting worse.

Mima Belford remembers fumigation and isolation procedures: It's not so long ago that if someone had scarlet fever the house was fumigated – you had to go out all that day to let the air settle – in the 1950s. I mind one of my boys took it and the other didn't and the nurse said 'It'll be your turn next'. We went to the hospital to see the youngest and if you'd any children you'd to stand at the gate outside and look through the glass window.

This aspect of life is one that people are thankful to see in the past, with a dramatic decline in mortality from these diseases since the middle of the twentieth century.

11

Till Death Us Do Part

'You may pass this way but once ...'

Before the advent of a universal old-age pension at a reasonable level in the 1960s, people who had worked all their lives could find themselves struggling financially in old age. Retirement was seen as a few quiet years before the inevitability of death.

During the first half of the twentieth century death was an accepted part of life in the tenements. Although it was associated with a number of superstitions, it was not taboo. Slipping away with your family round you or knowing that your body would be laid out at home to be visited by friends and relations before being taken away to be buried was a comforting thought to the dying, while for the family it was an extension of the tenement belief in looking after your own. The wake after a funeral could be a celebratory occasion.

OLD AGE

Women after years of childbearing and hard labour in the home were often prematurely aged, like Mary Gilchrist's mother-in-law. They all looked old even at fifty. Even my mother-in-law was an old lady. When I first saw her she must have been fifty. Dressed in dark green, maroon or black and in the afternoon, what she called a 'diddly' a wee fancy apron ... If she saw bright colours she'd say, 'Oh, not for me. Mutton dressed as lamb.'

Most men who reached retirement age did not live long to enjoy it: women often outlived their partners. As Jean Hay recalls: My grandfather only lived two years after he retired. Retirement seemed to cut them down. Seventy-two he was, but my grandmother was ninety-one when she died.

Responsibility for looking after elderly parents was generally accepted as part of a cycle of life by children who had once themselves been dependent on their mother and father. This is the burden of a rhyme which a Glasgow woman's father used to recite:

171

My boy it's your Father and Mother
Who nursed you in days gone by,
Do not turn us from the door
Out in the streets to die.
Remember the days of your childhood
When you prattled around our knees.
Don't be unthankful in our old age,
Remember your Mother and me.

Daughters conventionally took on the task of caring, going home to help their mothers with the housework as Betty Hepburn did. You know long ago, mums and daughters and sons, you all stayed more or less close together. Although you were married and left home and had the appliances to make it easier, you still went back home and scrubbed the stair when it was your mum's turn to do the stair. You took her washing away, you washed down the paintwork. The little time you had, you went back and helped at home 'cos they were getting older and needed a wee hand. I don't say that gadgets made our life any easier, because you all had your different things to do as you got older, you did more things for your mum, or you had a sick aunt or your granny to go and look after.

Even if women had houses on the new schemes, they often travelled into the older areas of the city to help their parents, as Jane Patterson says, speaking of the years after the Second World War: You see, they would come from their nice local authority house to the old house in the centre of town, where the old parents were living, and do their shopping and do their washing and all that.

Infirm parents often went to live with their grown children. The alternative was the ignominy of the poorhouse, as Bette Stivens makes clear: In parents' and grandparents' time no matter what size your house was, granny would come to stay. It was that or the poorshoose: Queensberry House, Craiglockhart, Inverleith – all were poorhouses. It was a terrible thing to go to the poorshoose ... It meant your family didn't care, nobody cared. You were just a nonentity, abandoned. That's what people thought in the Twenties or Thirties. *John Sinclair of Edinburgh remembers the fear his mother had of the poorhouse.* There was Queensberry House in the Canongate. My mother said, 'You can put me in any home, but don't put me in Queensberry House!' It had a bad name, a stigma! They had it in their mind and

55. An elderly couple in Springburn, Glasgow, 1970s: the fridge and television represent changes that made life easier than it had been for their parents.

you couldn't move it. *In Glasgow the main poorhouse was Barnhill near Springburn, which later became Foresthill Hospital.*

Some old people existed in appalling conditions on such handouts as were available from charitable organisations. Marald Grant, of the Guild of Aid in Glasgow, remembers one such old woman. There was a wee body. I forget what you called her but she used to live in the base-ment of a house opposite our front door, the Guild of Aid door. She was Granny something or another, Granny Robertson ... But this granny was the filthiest person I've ever seen in my life. One day she didn't come over when I sent the word ... and there was no answer and they were banging away at the door, and when I went over we opened the door and she was dead. Lying in the middle of sacks or rags. She was just dead on the floor. Really I've never seen such poverty.

Children with special needs could be left alone and unable to cope after an elderly parent died. Anne Campbell remembers an old woman in Hill-side Street, Edinburgh who had been the carer for her adult son. I re-member a knock on the door and it was her son, clearly agitated. He kept saying, there's something wrong with my mother, there's something wrong with my mother. ... They had the basement flat, and mother was clearly dead, sitting upright in a chair and had been dead for some time. They took her away, still sitting in the chair, she was still upright, and her son didn't seem to understand. Just said, he said, 'the funniest thing is the budgie just keeled over as well. At exactly the same time'. He found it really hard to look after himself after that. Would buy three fish suppers at a time to last a few days and would heat them up. Just lived down the road from the chippie as well.

Married couples inevitably have to face life alone when one or other of them dies: Mary Holligan expresses the pain of loss. One thinks they are going to be there forever and then all of a sudden one is left. How we forgot to say things we should have, things that weren't said. One regrets a lot of things. I felt I had no freedom at all and then one day he was taken away. I've had plenty of time to think back ... I only knew his value and his company when it was too late. I have missed him terribly and more as I've got older.

When women's lives had been so much defined by marriage they would find it hard to build a new life beyond the home after the loss of a husband, as May Carson from Glasgow found. When one loses his or her partner nobody wants you. One tries to go to socials or clubs. Dances you sit alone as men are frightened for the wives who might think we would take them away.

In contrast with earlier generations, for many people growing old in the second half of the twentieth century, retirement lasts for several years, and people can remain active during this time. James Stuart Grahame expresses a positive view of old age. We have all the blessing of the old people's clubs, day centres and that, old time dancing and all that. Old people are still, they're young today. They refuse to grow old. Age is relative to your physical and mental condition. People refuse to grow old now.

PREPAREDNESS FOR DEATH

Dodo Keenan believes that her generation had a practical attitude to mortality. I think the young ones are less prepared for death. It used to be that after you got married you insured your mother and father and that was because you would have to take time off work when they died and you didnae get paid. *People lived with an awareness of death and by the mid twentieth century only the very poorest would have no insurance or burial plan. Children were insured from birth for 1d or 2d a week as Jean Hay recalls:* Your mother took out penny policies from the day you were born. At five years old she increased it up to two pence. I've got about four but they are all paid up now.

Funeral parlours offered prospective customers and their families plans spread over months or years. The Co-operative Society in both Glasgow and Edinburgh provided funerals that could be paid up in advance. It was a matter of pride for people to know that they were not going to be a burden in death to relatives. There was widespread horror of the indignity of a pauper's funeral, which suggested worthlessness, as Dodo Keenan implies: Then there were the Paupers' Ground – they were never acknowledged. They used orange box wood for coffins.

Despite the seriousness of the subject there was graveyard humour associated with funeral parlours: 'Go to Harkess, he'll bury your carcass' *was said about one Edinburgh undertaker, while, as George Flannigan remembers, Stoddart in Great Junction Street, Edinburgh had a notice in the window:* 'You may pass this way but once but we'll get you in the end'. *Local undertakers would be familiar figures within the community. Rita Flannigan remembers the Stoddarts:* Right undertakers – tall and angular and wore black suits and hats, they used to stand at the door and watch the world go by.

Families would often buy a burial plot well before they needed it. Graveyard plots could provide burial space for several members of a family. People like Greta Connor could live their lives knowing where their last resting-place would be. When my dad died and we went to get a granite stone, my mum said 'Don't space out the lettering too much because you'll need to leave a space for Greta!' I've got a lair of ground, I know where I'm going to be buried, but I was thinking of going to see the undertaker and make arrangements. I mean it's no a foolish thing tae think about, just to see what the cost is.

Dodo Keenan remembers a useful present: My sister-in-law's mother used to clean for the superintendent of Easter Road cemetery and when she retired she got a present of two lairs.

For Beth K. a family mother-in-law joke was attached to the plot. When my grandfather died they put him in the family plot which had room for four people. There was only a baby in there that had

175

been put in when the plot was opened up in about 1910 and she didn't count. Then my mother died and she went in. Then my granny a few weeks later. That left one space that my dad wanted, but he was really troubled at the thought of having his mother-in-law between them for all eternity!

A good death after a full life is what people aspired to, and a good send-off was a way of giving respect to the deceased and showing the world that those left behind were dutiful and respectable. To this end many families would virtually bankrupt themselves through fear of seeming too poor to afford a decent funeral. As the price of funerals rose more people began to consider cremation although it was uncommon in Scotland until after the Second World War. Dodo Keenan explains: When you bought your ground you got either three-lair or five-lair and if you still had ground you wouldnae go in the crematorium, but sometimes for all you had the ground, it was cheaper going to the crematorium.

The costs did not end with the funeral: people had to be seen to be looking after the grave or else risk social sanction. They might also have to pay for general upkeep of the cemetery. Joan Croal was caught when she visited a family grave in Edinburgh: The Ash Cash! I was at my great-grandfather's grave in Piershill – I was tracing my family tree and got inveigled into paying an annual fee for grass cutting. I am now paying £3 or £4 a year ... for my great-grandfather that I didn't even know.

DEATH AND GRIEVING

Adults approached the subject of mortality with a mixture of pragmatism, religion and superstition. Belief in the doctrine of original sin meant that babies had to be christened or their lives dedicated to God, but at the same time mothers would be extremely superstitious about 'tempting providence'. As one Glasgow woman said: In the early years of this century when a woman made the clothes for her baby, she usually made herself a shroud, because women died in childbirth. You were expected to lose one baby. They didn't choose to buy things until the baby was born. It was considered bad luck. Or else the clothes would be knitted but not sewn up and finished.

High infant mortality rates meant that during the first half of the twentieth century many parents might have to face burying a child.

Funeral parlours would sometimes demand payment up front, which made the experience particularly traumatic for Emily Batten from Edin-burgh, organising a funeral for her baby daughter, one of twins, who died at nine weeks old. My husband and I went to the funeral undertaker and we asked to have a funeral, and I says it's for a baby. He says, 'Well before ye start, I'll have tae tell ye that ye'll have to pay the money before the funeral', because he had been done out of so much money ... We were taken aback because we wisnae ... we weren't going to do that to the man. So my husband had been demobbed and he had the demob money. So we went to the bank, we got the money and we went back tae the undertaker's shop. And he gave us a receipt. And it was affy upsetting you know, having to carry on like that with such a thing happening. So we bought a bit ground in Seafield cemetery and it's still there yet, the bairn's the only one that's in it. The baby's in it – since 1946 when she died. She's in that bit of ground.

Babies were buried quietly, as Joan Williamson describes: A baby was always in a white coffin, not in a hearse at the door, just a cab. The minister would sit with the coffin on his knee. But I don't suppose there was as much looking at the baby before it went be-cause they were probably still-born or just a few months old.

A public display of emotion was not really the Lowland Scots way and people tended rather to contain their grief. As one Glasgow woman com-ments: My daughter had five miscarriages and a dead born baby. She has one wee girl and what happened was she has never dis-cussed it with me. *Christine Quarrell's first baby died at just a few months old:* After the baby died I was not allowed to grieve in the main. For my family and the people around me the pain was too great ... And then being all in black at seventeen.

However Helen Nickerson remembers how her mother grieved at the loss of her son Harry. My mother went berserk. My mother was awfy ill when my brother Harry died because that was the oldest laddie and there was nae ... it was the most unexpected laddie be-cause she never thought for a minute she'd lose him. And that was in 8 Argyle Street and she thought my dad didna bother cos he used to go down for his pints and that ... And then she was sitting one night and the candle went out ... She had the candle and the candle was going down and she was sitting at the table and she said Harry came to her and said, 'Look Ma, dinnae greet like that for me because I'm happy', and from then on my mother bucked up ... but she never really got over Harry.

Children were encouraged to view the body as a way of taking the fear out of death. Greta Connor recalls her mother's views. When I was a wee lassie the girl next door died. ... My mother explained it to me, no' like a frightening thing. She believed that if you could even touch the forehead of the dead person it calmed ye down and so it does. The coolness of them calms your fear. *Betty Hepburn also recalls being taken in to see a dead child.* They used to dress them up beautifully. I must have been about five, starting school, and one of our wee playmates died and we were all taken in one at a time and she was dressed and had all her bows in her hair and her face had been made up and she had her party dress on and we saw her as an angel and then we all had to sing 'Jesus Loves Me' and then we came out. That was her away to heaven and it didn't affect us. There really was nothing frightening because the undertaker made them look quite pleasant. Otherwise, the lid was closed if they'd died a horrific death.

Margaret McDonald was only a child when she had the terrifying experience of losing her father, her mother having died some years earlier. I remember the night my father died. It was bronchitis. Myself and the brother were in the house and he took not well and called the doctor out. He prescribed him something but he wasn't getting any better. We had to call him out again around 10.30 that night and the doctor came out and told us my father had gone. We were screaming and going mad. The next minute the doctor must have radioed for police because they were everywhere because it was two juvenile children in the house. We then had to go to some neighbour's house because the morgue van was coming to take my father away and that wasn't a nice sight. That itself was horrific.

Greta Connor's mother died very suddenly in the middle of her housework. My mother collapsed at the wash-tub and died. We didn't expect it. The first we knew of it was next morning. I was twenty-two. She lay in the house.

Washing and dressing her mother just before her death proved to be a last act of love and respect for Mary Holligan. I happened to go up one Saturday night as I lived round the corner, and she said to me 'I'm not long for this world, something kept telling me, and I want you to go to the Co-op and pay any bills that I'm owing them.' I started to cry as I hadn't any chums at all or people to take comfort in, so I tried to talk her out of it, and she said it won't take place right now but soon. So she told me and showed me her little will and birth certificates and her parent's marriage lines etcetera, all her instructions to be carried out at her death. She wanted there to be no mourning and no publicity either ...

When my mother died, although my dear husband was by my side, but I couldn't be consoled. It was a terrible trauma when she died so suddenly, as I had gone up the night before. I don't know to this day what made me do it, for I was shy with my mother, but I said to her 'Ma, I would like to comb your hair.' We were sitting by the fire and a friend called Cathy was in the house at the time. She, mother, had long hair but when I started to comb it all seemed to come out in large tufts. However it got combed and then I said I wanted to wash her face. She said, 'What's all this? I can do that myself.' But I got the water and washed her face, and she washed her hands herself. Then I went to her big wooden chest and got a clean white vest and a white night-dress and although I felt a bit awkward I put them on. Then she said to Cathy, 'You know Cathy, when Mary was a few months old she became ill with double pneumonia and was at death's door. She was getting poulticed back and front and at one point it was the crisis and the doctor said, "She'll be all right, she'll hold your head for you yet", and so she has, Cathy. And what is more she has laid me out ... Mum died a few hours later. I found her half in and half out of bed. I was glad she had been washed and changed as I didn't get the opportunity after. I couldn't settle. I felt so lost.

LAYING OUT

Before the process of preparing a body for burial shifted to the sphere of the funeral parlour, the laying out of the dead, like the delivering of babies, was usually attended to by a local woman, often a widow, as Betty Hepburn remembers: There was one wifie on our stair. She did anybody that died. She laid them out, and the other one, she delivered the babies. *Women might undertake this duty for their hus-*

bands, as Isa Flucker says: If the husband died the wife might do it if she was able. But I suppose if they were cut up about it and very sad there was always another woman who would come and do that.

Traditionally the body stayed in the house for up to three days before the funeral, in a coffin in the front room if there was one, or across chairs, or on the best bed, or even on the kitchen table, so friends and relatives could pay their respects. It was not uncommon for the deceased never to be left alone, with family members sitting in vigil, men often 'taking the night shift'. Joan Williamson recalls the inconvenience this created in a crowded house. I remember my grandad said, 'If ever anything happens to me, will you take me home?' And he meant 'when I die'. My granda did lay in the room there for all there were so many of us at home. My brothers had left the house but there were still four girls and a boy and we had to do while that was there and maybe stay with a friend. That was three days that my mother had to put up with that.

In a single end ordinary domestic life had to continue around the body, which might be shifted from bed to table or coal bunker: this was appalling to finer society, as is clear from evidence given by Mary Laird of the Women's Labour League to the Royal Commission on Housing in 1913. However the practice continued to be taken for granted in the tenements, as Bet Small recalls. In 1951 when my father died there was an aunt, my sister and myself in a single bed for three nights and my father was lying in the other bedroom in a double bed! *Greta Connor's mother, who died in 1967, was laid out in the house by an undertaker:* My mother died in the house and the undertaker came to the house, dressed her and she lay in the room with the blind drawn and the light on and people came to pay their respects.

Even if people died in hospital they would usually be brought home to be viewed. Dodo Keenan found no difficulty in sleeping in the same room as her mother's body, but her husband perhaps represented changing attitudes to this practice after the Second World War. Mostly they would bring them from the hospital unless you were awfy stuck for room. When my mother died in '46 my mother lay in the room and my sister and I slept there. But my husband would not go into that room. He mustn't have been brought up to see things like that ... We were brought up [to believe], they didn't do you any harm when they were alive, they'll no' do you any harm when they're dead.

The treatment of the dead mixed respect and the need to accept that the dead body is simply a shell left behind. Elsie Tierney has a vivid child's-eye memory of her grandmother. My granny had a lot of rheumatism before she died and had to keep her feet up in bed. When she died they had to break her legs and put a wringer over the top to keep them down. I must have been about six. I remember peeping round the door She was laid out in a coffin on three chairs. My mother must have slept in the room with her. They had an awful job getting Granny down the stair.

Some superstitions were observed. It was not uncommon for Glasgow folk, especially immigrants from the Highlands or Ireland, to leave a window open to allow the soul to leave. Mirrors might be covered so that the soul would not be confused as it set forth. Christine Quarrell remembered the priest trying to counter such superstitious behaviour in the 1960s. Some of my first husband's family were quite traditional and they came up and covered the mirrors and the priest told them that this was a baby, an innocent, and you don't do that.

Religious people might be taken to the church the night before the funeral. Before Cathy Cullen from Glasgow died in 1999 she had planned how she wanted her last night on earth to be. I want to be left in the church overnight. It is a special time, I'd rather be near to God in the church before I leave earth. That was where I was taken at the beginning of my life, and I'd like to think I'd return there at the end of my life.

THE FUNERAL

On the day of the funeral the coffin would be taken from the house or local church and the entire neighbourhood would be able to witness this last journey. Greta Connor expresses the general sense of community involvement. In our day living in a tenement you were living in each other's pockets anyway – their tragedy was your tragedy and wisnae a thing you could just shut your eyes to.

Funerals were a common sight for Joan Williamson: The kids in our street were quite used to seeing coffins and funeral hearses. The funeral undertakers had the stables in our street and had the

56. A typical funeral in Newhaven 1928. The family and main mourners walk behind the horse drawn hearse carrying the body of David Dryburgh Finlay. There were 600 mourners at his funeral.

broughams. They'd be down our street every day and the flowers that fell off, we'd collect and take them up to our house. I don't think we were frightened of these things. It was an everyday occurrence.

People would pay their respects and men would always remove their hats if a coffin came by. As Margaret Cullinan says, No car would overtake a funeral cortège, even to this day. *George Flannigan recalls:* When a funeral passed the traffic stopped and passers by acknowledged the funeral. *Norrie Campbell of Edinburgh recalls special gestures of respect at the funerals of well-known individuals:* Even the shopkeepers dropped their blinds. I remember when Fish Jean was being buried, she lived in Dorset Place and all the shopkeepers' blinds went down.

Neighbours would often hold a collection to buy flowers, as Dodo Keenan remembers: Someone always volunteered to go round with a

182

sheet and they knocked at each neighbour's door to get money for flowers. As often as not it was [an arrangement] termed a globe, with a glass cover. Many's a time they spent the money, and they were dear. The bereaved could have done with the money.

Emily Batten has a poignant memory of a wreath arriving too late for the funeral of her baby. After the funeral left the street a great big wreath was delivered tae the house. A beautiful wreath. But there was no way we could run after it or make other arrangements at that time. So my husband and I put the baby in the pram, and we waited until it was dark. It was November, it was November 5th that the baby died. It was a blooming cold, cold night. So we put the baby in the pram and wrapped the wreath up in a – I cannae mind how we done that now, it was a bag or something – and we put the wreath on top of the pram. And we walked all the way from Hamilton Street in Leith tae Seafield cemetery and it was a freezing cold night. And then we gets to the cemetery and we knocked on the superintendent's door and he came tae the door and I explained to him that this wreath had come from friends too late for the funeral and would he put it on the baby's grave. And we had to walk a' the way back. I was absolutely frozen. It was like a nightmare ... that cold night with me and my man and the bairn – the other twin – away along to the cemetery.

Funerals also brought their share of hangers-on. Isa Keith remembers an Edinburgh character who used to accompany hearses. I remember there used to be a man, Daft Sandy they called him. He used tae go to all the funerals, everybody's funeral. And he would walk along, they used tae walk mostly. There'd be a hearse and a lot of people walked. There wasnae so many cars ... maybe if it was a fancier funeral, somebody that had mair money there'd be cars but an awful lot more seemed to be walking, walking behind the cortège.

Horse-drawn funerals were remembered by Joan Williamson. Lovely horses with black plumes and you all walked behind. That was a walking funeral. There was always a brougham and two carriages. It was only the main mourners that went into the carriage. Everyone else walked.

Surviving from Victorian times were rules governing appropriate dress. People were expected to wear black as a sign of mourning, as Greta

Conner recalls. We wore black for maybe six months. And you were pitied if you didn't. Poor soul. Fancy! Didn't even have black. There was an old comedian who sang a song criticising someone going to a funeral in black suit and brown boots.

Among tenement folk burying the dead was always a man's job – women did not attend the committal, as May Carson remarks: Women never used to go to funerals, you see. Not in they days. It wisnae common among our lot anyway – working people. The women just didnae seem to go to funerals, tae the actual taking it to the cemetery. They maybe went to the church, to the service but they didnae seem to go wi' the body to the cemetery.

This must have hindered the process of grieving for some women. Mary MacKay's sister broke this convention. My sister attended my mother's funeral. She insisted on going. She was the only female there.

AFTERWARDS

Women might go to the church but otherwise would stay at home and prepare a funeral tea, something like ham sandwiches or steak pie. In most cases, as Mima Belford describes, there was a drink on offer. The usual ritual was that you went back to the house after the funeral and had a knees-up. There was a lot of people went to funerals to get that. And the men always got a dram because they were so cold standing at the cemetery. It was to heat them up. The women might have sherry or port.

Because of poverty the funeral of Helen Nickerson's brother Harry was a simple and inexpensive affair. Her father, a fisherman, had to return quickly to his boat. We were that poor that it was jist family, her ain bairns and maybe a neighbour, Mrs Baird, that came into the house to help her, but she done all the arrangement herself with my father and they had to bring him home from the trawlers ... he was that hard up ... we were all hard up so he had to go back to the boat. On the day of the funeral they just had a cup of tea and a bun. He was buried. There wasnae such a thing as cremated in they days. It was a' burials. She had to pay the money for a bit of ground and she had to bury Harry and then she slipped Stuart and Roy both in the same grave. It was a really hard life for her.

Religion could help people cope with grief. Attending church at least meant that people were not alone, and allowed for those left behind to feel pride. People in the tenement might not always be religious but they had been brought up god-fearing and never was this more apparent than at the time of a death in the family. May Hutton was grateful to her local minister for the way he handled things. We've got an awfy good minister ... he's a very good man. He was awfy good to me when Freddy died. He raked up everything about Freddy and spoke about it. A lovely service and life just goes on after that.

The bereaved have to learn to live with the empty feeling in the house and certain objects such as father's chair have a particular resonance. Margaret McDonald recalls constantly expecting to see her mother in her usual place in the home. I was coming in from work half expecting to see her from the night shift. She used to have my porridge on and I used to tell her not to talk to me first thing in the morning. I found the night-time the worst time though. I could sleep in my mother's single bed but I couldn't sleep on my own and look into her single bed ... What can you do though? It is life.

Medical advances and the benefits of a more affluent society mean that people are living longer, and death is perhaps becoming more taboo than it was in the period remembered in these pages. Death may come in the end, but until it does, old people in good health can enjoy some of the pleasures of their earlier life. James Stuart Grahame is one who speaks of living life to the full. You would be surprised when you see us men and women at the clubs. We're just like laddies and lassies. We carry on just like young people.

Appendix on Prices and Wages

Before the change to the decimal system of British currency in 1971, there were 20 shillings in a pound and 12 pennies or pence in a shilling. With decimalisation one shilling became 5 new pence (5p), two shillings 10p and 10 shillings 50p. So for example 'two and six' (2s 6d) in old money was the equivalent of $12^{1}/_{2}$p.

Of course in real terms the value of money has changed greatly. As a rough idea, £1 at the time of writing was worth the following amounts (which fluctuated through the decades) at these marker points in the period we are considering:

1910	£53.88
1920	£20.03
1930	£31.56
1940	£27.12
1950	£21.51
1960	£14.45

(Data kindly supplied by Neil Arora, Bank of England.)

As a witness before the Royal Commission on Housing in 1913, Mary Laird of the Women's Labour League handed in a statement that included the following weekly budget for a family consisting of husband, wife and three children aged six, nine and twelve years. The husband's wages were 32 shillings (£1.60p) a week.

| *Housekeeping bill* | Per Week | |
	s	d
10 loaves at 3d	2	6
1 lb butter at 1s 3d	1	3
2lbs margarine at 8d	1	4
2lb jar jam at $7^{1}/_{2}$d	0	$7^{1}/_{2}$
3lbs sugar at $2^{1}/_{2}$d	0	$7^{1}/_{2}$
1lb haddocks at $4^{1}/_{2}$d	0	$4^{1}/_{2}$
2 stone potatoes at 8d	1	4
$^{1}/_{4}$ stone meal at 2s 4d	0	7

Beef at 7d a day	4	1
Milk at 2d a day	1	2
Vegetables 1d a day	0	7
6oz tea at 1s 8d	0	$7^1/_2$
1 pair kippers or $^1/_4$lb cheese at $2^1/_2$d	0	$2^1/_2$
Soap $2^1/_2$d; powder 1d	0	$3^1/_2$
Sticks $1^1/_2$d; matches $^1/_2$d	0	2
Pepper, salt, black lead, emery, polish	0	2
	15	11

Per week	s	d
Rent	6	0
Coal, 2 bags at 1s 1d	2	2
Gas	0	7
Husband's pocket money	1	6
Children's pocket money	0	3
Church seats	0	3
Church subscription	0	$1^1/_2$
Church collection	0	$3^1/_2$
Societies–Friendly, 6d;		
Nat. Insurance, 4d	0	10
Funeral, husband 2d, wife		
and children each 1d	0	6
Clothes for husband	1	0
Clothes for wife	1	0
Clothes for children	1	6
	16	0
Housekeeping	15	11
Total	31	11

Glossary

aye	*always*
back court/green	*an enclosed area behind a tenement used for drying clothes, etc.*
blether	*gossip, chat*
Buroo	*Labour Exchange*
close	*shared entry passage to a tenement building (Glasgow); a passage way or alley usually between tenements (Edinburgh)*
cludgie	*toilet*
flit	*move from a house*
greet	*cry*
gub	*mouth*
guising	*dressing up for Hallowe'en etc.*
heid	*head*
hough	*hock*
ken	*know*
lair	*a burial space or grave*
menage	*a privately organised savings club*
messages	*shopping*
piece	*a piece of bread or sandwich*
the room	*parlour/bedroom in a room-and-kitchen house*
press	*cupboard*
single end	*a one-room house*
steamie	*public wash house (Glasgow)*
tatties/totties	*potatoes*
tumshee	*turnip*
wally	*ceramic, glazed earthenware*
wean	*child*
winching	*wenching, chasing girls*

Selected Reading

Community Service Volunteers, *A Patchwork of Memories*, Edinburgh, 1996

Faley, Jean, *Up Oor Close: Memories of Domestic Life in Glasgow Tenements, 1910-1945*, Wendlebury, 1990

Glasser, Ralph, *Growing up in the Gorbals*, London, 1986

Reid, J. M., *Homeward Journey*, Edinburgh, 1988

Report of the Royal Commission on the Housing of the Industrial Population of Scotland, Rural and Urban, 1917 (The Commission was set up in 1912 to investigate housing, but because of the First World War did not report until 1917.)

Ritchie, James T. R., *The Singing Street*, Edinburgh & London, 1964

Rountree, G., *A Govan Childhood in The Nineteen Thirties*, Edinburgh, 1993

Tait, H. P., *A Doctor and Two Policemen: The History of Edinburgh Public Health Department 1862-1974*, Edinburgh, 1974

Weir, Molly, *Shoes Were For Sunday*, London, 1970

Wilkinson, R., *Memories of Maryhill*, Edinburgh, 1993

Wordsall, Frank, *The Glasgow Tenement: A Way of Life*, Glasgow, 2nd edn 1989

Workers' Educational Association, *Kiss Me While My Lips Are Tacky*, Edinburgh, 1988

Workers' Educational Association, *Friday Night Was Brasso Night*, Edinburgh, 1987

Index

Italicised page numbers refer to illustrations

Up Oor Close
Memories of Domestic Life in Glasgow Tenements 1910–1945

Jean Faley

This popular book explores the rich fabric of working-class home life through the recollections of people who grew up in these one- and two-room houses.

If Glasgow tenements summon up images of dereliction and slum poverty *Up Oor Close* will be an eye-opener. Drawn largely from the

oral history archives of Springburn Museum, the book is full of detail and stories which illuminate the experience of tenement life – from shopping and housework to childbirth and death. The routines and rituals which maintained respectable standards in conditions unimaginable today are vividly recorded. A fascinating book for readers of all ages.

ISBN 0 9513124 5 6 pb
176 pp., 45 b&w ill., 216 x 138 mm, 1990

For other titles please visit our website, www.whitecockade.co.uk.